Presented to

From

Date

DREAM SEER

Searching for the Face of the Invisible

Barbie L. Breathitt, Ph.D.

Books by Dr. Barbie L. Breathitt

Dream Encounters: Seeing Your Destiny from God's Perspective

Gateway to the Seer Realm: Look Again to See Beyond the Natural

So You Want to Change the World?

Hearing and Understanding the Voice of God

Dream Seer: Searching for the Face of the Invisible

Dream Interpreter

A to Z Dream Symbology Dictionary

Volume I Dream Symbols

Volume II Dream Symbols

Volume III Dream Symbols

Action Dream Symbols

When Will My Dreams Come True? Dream Interpretation Nuggets, Times & Seasons

Dream Sexology

Sports & Recreation Dream Symbols

Breath of the Spirit Ministries, Inc.
P.O. Box 820653
North Richland Hills, Texas 76182–0653
www.BarbieBreathitt.com
www.BarbieBreathittEnterprises.com
www.MyOnar.com

ISBN-13: 978-1-60-383257-2

Published by: Barbie Breathitt Enterprises, Inc.

Printed in Canada

Dedication

DREAM SEER Searching for the Face of the Invisible is dedicated to my loving brother Steven Alan Breathitt. Saved at the age of five, Steven has always searched for the face of God. He faithfully served on staff at a mega church and it took three people to replace him when he moved to administrate Breath of the Spirit in Texas. He has tirelessly grown and developed the ministry to the place it is today. Steven has been my inspiration, constant friend, confidant, and advisor through the thick battles with thin enumerations. He shared in the glorious mountain top experiences as well as walking through life's dark valleys. He has picked me up, lending his strength when I needed fortifying, letting me lean on him when weary, and encouraging me while the trials of life seemed too much to bear. He coaxed me onward to achieve God's highest call for my life. When God's blessings were too many to count, he celebrated His goodness. Being a true servant of God Steven has always taken the higher road, the narrow way less traveled, even if he had to walk it alone. Steven is content to rest in the shadows to ensure that others shine from the platform when he is more talented and gifted than most. Steven is a gentle man who does not seek the world's applause or the limelight of fame. He is full of wisdom, love, wit and the compassion of God. He is a good listener because he listens from the heart. But, more importantly, Steven is a man of God, full of integrity, who hears the voice of God, counts the cost, gives up his personal dreams for others, and gladly follows the Holy Spirit wherever and whenever He leads.

Endorsements

Most of us who are true believers want to hear the voice of God when He has something to say to us. However, Barbie Breathitt, through her fascinating book Dream Seer, has alerted me to the fact that I might be missing some of what God has been saying because I have not been properly tuned into the wavelengths of my dreams. This persuasive book takes people like me into new realms of reality, namely how God uses our dream life to hear His voice more clearly, to be activated into new levels of service, and to fulfill His destiny for us. After you read Dream Seer you will never be the same!

C. Peter Wagner
Vice-President Global Spheres, Inc.

I want to highly recommend to you this amazing new book by Barbie Breathitt called the Dream Seer. In her book Barbie shares incredible revelation and insight into the understanding and function of the world of dreams. As a leading voice in the Body of Christ in Dreams and interpretation, and understanding dream language, Barbie brings a fresh revelation that is easy to understand and digest. I want to highly recommend this book for all church leaders and those with supernatural schools who are hungry for more and are looking to teach and bring understanding into the realm of seeing into the Supernatural Kingdom of God. This is a must read!

Jeff Jansen
Global Fire Ministries International
Senior Leader Global Fire Church
Global Connect Churches
Kingdom Life Institute

Barbie Breathitt of Breath of the Spirit Ministries has done it again! Few people I know can merge together such bodies of truth and convey it in such a manner that the everyday person can comprehend. In the book Dream Seer, Searching for the Face of the Invisible, Barbie takes you on a journey that is deep and wide at the same time. By combining understanding from scripture, physiological truths, the science of the brain all with a prophetic edge that penetrates any resistance. Well done! Amazing!

James Goll
Encounters Network • Prayer Storm • God Encounters Training
Best Selling Author of The Seer, The Lost Art of Intercession,
Dream Language and many more.

Barbie Breathitt does an excellent job of linking the move of God in our lives with the dreams that He places in us. Barbie uncovers for us God's divine revelation of who each of us have been destined to be! Your life-dreams will be unraveled and made clear, for she writes as a prophetic sage, full of wisdom gained through years of experience. Dream Seer will show you that your life has been created to experience God, and Barbie will show you how! Sprinkled with true life stories that will capture your attention she brings before you the power of spiritual transformation from a godly perspective. Curious about your destiny and the path God has placed you on? Then DREAM SEER is for you! Read it and enjoy the journey!

Dr. Brian Simmons
Stairway Ministries & The Passion Translation Project

I believe Barbie Breathitt's new book, Dream Seer, will stir you to pursue the things of the spirit with a hunger to hear the voice of God through Dreams and Visions. She writes that Dreams have the power to awaken us to our destiny. This book is a revelatory key that will certainly empower you to be led by the Spirit and to help fulfill the will of God in your life.

Adam F Thompson
Co-Author of "The Divinity Code to Understanding Your Dreams & Visions"
www.thedivinitycode.org
Co-Planter of "Field of Dreams Australia"
www.fieldofdreams.org.au

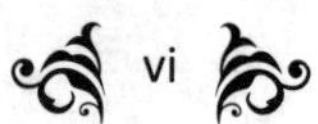

Barbie's book, Dream Seer, is a topically-packed handbook filled with insights that empower the reader to better understand and participate with God in seeing their dreams become reality. In this book she also imparts wisdom and revelation beyond mere dream interpretation to see champions raised for the kingdom. A must read for all hungry to see heaven on earth.

Adrian Beale
Co-Author of "The Divinity Code to Understanding Your Dreams & Visions"
www.thedivinitycode.org
www.everrestministries.com

Dream Seer is an in-depth study tool, skillfully including the subjects of dreams and the seer anointing from a biblical perspective. It is EXCELLENT! This book is a must for your library. Those who sit under Barbie Breathitt's empowering prophetic teaching ministry gain a great increase in their understanding of how God speaks through revelations, dreams, and visions. The seer anointing is bound to awaken in your life as you read Dream Seer, Searching for the Face of the Invisible.

Patricia King
Founder, XPministries

Within the pages of this book Dr. Barbie Breathitt effectively takes us on a journey of unlocking prophetic gifts of God within us. She has the ability to impart to us the depth of wisdom and divine understanding she has gleaned over the years of proven prophetic ministry. You will be supernaturally stirred, gain deeper insight, be filled with Spirit-breathed vision and have many "ah ha" moments as you read. "I highly recommend this revelatory resource. It should be a part of every spiritual seeker library– I've already made it part of mine!"

Joshua Mills
Best Selling Author of "31 Days to a Miracle Mindset"
Palm Springs, Canada, California and London
www.JoshuaMills.com

Barbie's life's work in the ministry thus far can be summarized in two words: inhaling & exhaling... Inhaling a vast amount of scripture and study and exhaling a prolific volume of teachings and blessings. The multitudes that have been touched by her ministry are impressive and the testimonies are real. My hope and prayer is that this book will touch YOU.

Karl Zimmerman
Senior Wealth Advisor
Director of Wealth Management
Oakville, Ontario

Table of Contents

Foreword

In every circumstance we are in, we must find God's sovereignty in that circumstance and be faithful to walk in His will. One of the primary ways that God has always used to communicate with His people is through dreams and visions, yet they are often misunderstood, dismissed, or ignored. Dreams particularly can seem foolish or strange. In 1 Cor. 1:27, Paul said that God chose the foolish things of the world to confound the wise. Although many dreams are foolish or senseless to the world, they are precious to those who understand 'the hidden wisdom' from above.

The Old Testament is laden with dream scenes and interpretations. In the Bible we actually find over 50 references for messages being sent by God through dreams and visions, to both the righteous and the unrighteous alike. The Lord used dreams and visions to guide, to warn, to direct, to help – to communicate His heart. God has not stopped communicating to humanity by these means. In fact, God often uses dreams and visions to reach unsaved individuals with the Gospel, particularly in closed parts of the world. We have scores of testimonies of dreams and visions being used by God to draw individuals, families, and entire communities to Himself. Similarly, the Lord uses this method of revelation in the lives of most, if not all, believers.

What is a Dream?

A dream is a release of revelation (whether natural or spiritual) that comes at a time when your body is at peace and you are settled. Sometimes this is the only way God can communicate with us, because our soul is quiet enough for the Lord to speak deeply into our spirit man. A dream is like a photograph of something you are able to relate to in a movie form. Ecclesiastes 5:3 tells us that a dream comes when there are many cares.

Dreams are formed in a person's subconscious mind. They are based on the imagery and secret symbolic language that are exclusive and strategic to that person's particular life and destiny. Dreams can either be a subconscious response to the circumstances of our lives or the Holy Spirit communicating His plans, ways and purposes to us. Dreams enable us to tap into the superior ways of the Divine Spirit. Dreams enable us to glance into the imperceptible realms of wisdom, counsel, knowledge and might.

The dreams and visions God births in us bring revelation, illumination, and inspiration. When we accept delivery of God's dream letters of love, He releases the strategic power to change every life event into something wonderful. He turns negative happenings to our advantage and improvement. Dreams enable us to glance into the imperceptible realms of wisdom, counsel, knowledge and might.

Dreams Can Reveal the Future

In the ancient eastern world, dreams were treated as reality. Dreams were the world of the divine or the demonic. They often revealed the future. Dreams could be filled with revelation that would cause the dreamer to make the right decision for his/her future. For instance, I once had a dream because I was in prayer over a trip to Israel. Barbara Byerly and I were going to be leading prayer for a meeting that would reconcile Arab Christian leaders and Messianic leaders. Dr. Peter Wagner was going to be facilitating this meeting. There was much warfare surrounding this meeting. I became very anxious and called Barbara and told her we should pray and fast for three days before going. Barbara was having the same burden and agreed immediately.

In the second day of the fast I fell asleep and had the following dream: Barbara Wentroble, a well-known prophetess, was in the dream and asked me a question. "So, you are going to Israel. There are two ways. Which way are you taking?" I told her the way we were going. In the dream it was as if I was showing her a map and we were wandering through the Arab desert to get to Israel. She then said, "You may go that way, but if you do, you will experience much warfare. There is a better way for you to take." I said, "Oh, what is that way?" She replied, "Go straight to Israel and meet with the leadership you know. Then, have your meeting with everyone else." I woke up and knew I had revelation that God had spoken to me to give me direction for Dr. Wagner as he proceeded in pulling together this meeting. I encouraged him to first have a meeting with the leaders of Israel that we knew. Then we could have the overall meeting and reconciliation time. This proved to be straight revelation from God and really affected the overall outcome of our mission.

Israel was forbidden to use many of the same type of divining practices as Egypt and other neighboring countries and peoples. However, God would visit them in the night to communicate His will and way to them. This continued through the changing of covenants, from old to new. In the first two chapters of the New Testament, God gives direction through prophetic dreams five times.

Always Talk to God About Your Dreams

Exercising discernment is very important in determining the source of dreams and visions. Without this, we can be basing our life decisions on soulish desires, or the enemy could gain a ready inroad to thwart us in our destiny. No matter what the origin of a dream we have had, we can and should always talk to the Lord about what we have dreamed. Prophets such as Jeremiah and Zechariah cautioned about dreams not being filled with God's word (see Jer. 23:25–27; Zech.10:2). Jeremiah placed dreamers with soothsayers, sorcerers and false prophets (see Jer. 27:9). Therefore, he equated some dreams to false prophecy. God was warning through the prophets that people could begin to rely on dreams and not seek God's word for truth. So, not only could God reveal His will through dreams, but there was a warning not to just rely on this method to know the will of God.

We should not ignore what a dream may reveal about our emotions, and can always ask God to clarify puzzling or disturbing dreams so He can bring His comfort and healing to our mind, will, and emotions. If we discern that a dream is demonic in nature, it might be an indication of how the enemy is working to thwart us, or could be a call to a new level of spiritual warfare. All dreams have some level of significance in our lives, and it is important to invite the Lord into the process of determining what the level of significance of each dream may be. That is why the book you are holding in your hands is so valuable!

Barbie Breathitt is one of the best teachers there is on dream interpretation, and for decoding the symbols and code the Lord can use when communicating with His people. Her latest book, Dream Seer: Searching for the Face of the Invisible, will encourage you to believe your destiny is designed in the language of your dreams, visions and imagination, so anything is possible when God is present. God fashioned His glorious image, splendid character and grand imagination within each Believer so that our identity and nature is caught up in Christ. When our hearts feel God's emotions and our minds mirror His thoughts, we live and move in His presence to become a reflection of His greatness on earth.

As Barbie shares, dreams enable us to see the plans and purposes God had for us before we entered into this earthly realm of existence. All of our days were numbered and ordered before we were born. Part of our spiritual journey is learning how to enter into the divine scripts of success that have already been written for each of us in our dreams. Dreams bring the revelation of who we are to become in Christ once our spirit is awakened, our soul is born again, and then enlightened by the Holy Spirit. This revelation enables each believer to work together as a unit, while keeping our individuality. We each have a component and diverse function that is displayed through the corporate body of Christ, in the progression of life.

Dreams awaken our mind's vision to the unlimited possibilities that await us. Nothing is impossible when we attach ourselves to the power of God's love. We are created in God's image. Therefore, we possess the same power to create with our visual images and words. The dreams we envision grant us agreement with Heaven to remove any obstacle that would constrain us to be common. Dream Seer will cause a dimension of your seeing through night visions and dreams to come alive. As you read this book, expect to find yourself walking and living in a faith realm BEYOND where you have ever been before!

Dr. Chuck D. Pierce
President, Global Spheres Inc.
President, Glory of Zion Intl.

Introduction

Are dreams just a figment of our imagination or a fanciful desire that will never be realized? Are the dreams we dream just a way our subconscious deals with the business of the day? Or, do dreams really come true? And if they come true, when are they going to come true? How are dreams used to point to our future and destiny? Where does the motivation for astounding ideas come from? Is there a universal source that releases the ability to birth greatness or emboldens individuals to discover success and influence in life? Could it be that only a select unique few possess this gift? Or, has God granted humanity the ability to tap into the infinite realms of counsel, guidance and wisdom if they will only seek the face of an invisible God? The answers await us in the mysterious realms of the renewed mind and imagination. God has given us the power of imagination so that we can create an amazing life.

Dreams have the power to awaken us to destiny because they are guiding memories from God, the creator of the universe. Dream vapors reveal divine strategies and enlighten us to God's perfect plans. It is important that we trust in the pictures and images of our dreams. Dreams enable you to trust in what no one else can see but you. Your dreams give a personal, private viewing of the grand plans and the landscapes of success that are available for you to apprehend. It is important that you become an active participant in making your dreams a reality. Don't just take the attitude that if my dream is real, someday it will just happen on its own accord. You alone are called to take responsibility for the stewarding and mastery of the visions shown in your dreams.

Nothing in life that is worth its salt just happens. Life requires an investment of passion, hard work, and tears if we are to advance to a certain level of success. When I think about becoming successful, to me, it means the ability to fulfill the purpose for which a person was created. It is necessary to be diligent to make your dreams come true. The measure of dream fulfillment you experience will be directly related to the amount of time and effort you devote to understanding your dreams to insure that your dreams manifest. Always contend for the divine intervention your dreams are calling you to apprehend. When we realize that our steps are ordered by God, our confidence will rise to a new height of trust.

The symbols that fill our dreams paint a picture of what God wants to transpire in our lives if we will only believe Him for greatness. Faith enables the pictures to begin to form into tangible objects of reality. When our lives are over, God signs His name to the beautiful canvas of our existence. Then God proudly displays His workmanship in the art gallery of heaven. The colorful masterpieces He painted both shows and tells each of our stories.

The ethereal vapors of our dreams will become substantial presences when we believe that anything is possible with God. God is the giver of dreams. Jesus is also the Redeemer. So, like a knight in shining armor, He comes to restore the dreams we have allowed to fall by the wayside. The Holy Spirit inspires us to recall the images He sent long ago. God has mapped out our future. He brings the events of the world to bear on our individual circumstances as He wills. When the events of our lives coincide with the correct timing of His plans, the next phase of our destiny ensues. The Holy Spirit knows the perfect time to bring the dreams and plans He has formulated to enable our purpose to come to pass.

God knows the potential He has placed within every individual. So He creates the impossible dream that draws the very best out of us. During the inception of our destiny and at life's crossroads, God recreates the person's moral fiber, empowering them to fulfill the dreams He has given. God places His glorious image and grand imagination within us. God fashions His splendid character in us, so our identity and nature is caught up in Christ. When our heart feels His emotions and our mind mirrors His thoughts, we become a reflection of His greatness on earth. God has been acting from infinity to prepare us to succeed for eternity.

Chapter 1
Darkness into Light

Greatness is birthed in the darkest recesses of our soul. The extraction of this precious oil requires a season of pressure, pain and a desperate search for the light of God's truth. Only when the necessary changes have taken place within the soul, will the anointing that reflects God's glory bubble to the surface.

God conceals Himself in darkness so we are not able to discern the movement of His hands, though they are always at work on our behalf. God gets angry at our sin, not at us; because He knows our sin causes tears of regret to flow when we miss the highest goal, settling for less than He desires. God's anger only last for a solitary moment in the night. Once Holy Spirit's truth is discovered and embraced, God's favor brings great joy at the rising of the morning sun.

We are called to see, apprehend and continually experience God's loving kindnesses. We gain much wisdom through the depths of the process that God works into us in the valley of the shadow of death. His grace enables us to die to self, surrender to His perfect will and learn to walk in His higher ways. God desires to cut the chains that bind us, to release the burdens we carry and the things that weigh us down. When we yield to the pruning we will exit the dark night of the soul, enlightened to a new day, understanding that as we draw closer to knowing God and His redemptive ways, His light will now shine brighter in us than in our past.

Jesus, the Creator of all, hung naked surrounded in total darkness on the cross dying for the sins of the world; past, present and future. Gross darkness covered the entire earth from the sixth hour until the ninth hour. Even when Jesus was beaten beyond recognition and shrouded in obscurity, God knew exactly where Jesus was. God turned His face away from Jesus so not to look upon the sin Jesus bore for us. When Jesus freely gave His life, was nailed captive to a cross, blinded by a thick veil of gloom and the bitter pain of separation, God knew the divine plan and narrow path where He was leading Jesus for all of eternity. The crucifixion of Jesus was the darkest moment in history followed by the utmost resurrection light the world has ever known when He arose from the dead.

God searches the recesses of our hearts and tests every one to show us what resides within. God knows us completely; yet He is too wonderful and amazing for us to understand. He intently watches our every move and counts our every breath. He knows our steps and understands our very thought processes. God has formed and recorded the words we speak before they are uttered. God has scrutinized our path. He is intimately acquainted with all our ways. He knows when we sit, stand or lay down to rest. God guards and encloses us. He is always before, under, above and behind us at all times with His hand resting gently upon our shoulder.

When we are not able to see the next step, God promises His Word will be a light to forge our path. His Word will transform us and make us better when we emerge from the time of testing and the trying of our soul. Every test we take helps us learn to love. The person who does not love does not know the essence of God, for God is perfect love. God sent Jesus to manifest His love to a sinful world so we can be His children and have eternal life through Him.

God rewards a life of faith that trusts in Him. The praises of His children builds a spiritual habitation for the Lord. His presence brings deliverance, healing and peace. Our praise causes the Holy Spirit to move into our dilemmas so that His light of hope breaks forth in us. When our attention is drawn to the Kings' powerful countenance and we lift up our faces to see the light of His presence, God shines His love upon us. Our King beckons us to gaze full upon His lovely face. He loves us with an everlasting love. As a bridegroom rejoices over his bride so does the Lord rejoice over us.

When we gaze into God's affectionate eyes we can sense the tender love Jesus has for us. When lover's eyes meet they feel the depths of their passion for one another. Nothing is wasted in an infinite God who collects every one of our tears as a glistening treasure and stores them in a heavenly jar. God's compassion is touched by the feelings of our infirmities. Knowing the Holy Spirit has a divine dream plan, that He has never left or forsaken us, causes us to forget the times of intense pain and the years of suffering in darkness.

God controls everything; nothing is beyond His loving touch or wisdom. God does His deepest work during our darkest days. God is infinite light there is no darkness within Him at all. We are called to enter into God's presence to walk in God's penetrating light. When we are in the depths of the valley, we hear the distant thunder and the sound of the trumpets' call that brings fear to our heart. So we stand afar off and watch to see the lightening flash and the smoke rising from the mountain encounter of God. Instead of preparing ourselves to boldly rush in; we look for someone else to approach this holy God.

Moses, God's friend, drew near to God by passing through a cloud of thick darkness to enter God's radiant presence. Moses had to journey alone while the Israelites stood and shook in fear at a far distance. They were afraid to be tested, knowing that if they did not repent; their sinful condition would result in their death. They chose to stay in their rebellious condition and listen to a man speak on the behalf of God instead of making the dark cleansing journey into the light of God's presence. The light of God dwells in thick darkness; to see the countenance of His face, one must press in behind the veil. Exodus 20

Computer Software Shows the Face of the Heart

Date: June 7, 2014 Wake time: 5:48 a.m. Matthew 5:48, "Therefore you are to be perfect, as your heavenly Father is perfect."

In my dream I was part of the generation who sought to see the face of Jesus. I saw a computer simulator that had the ability to show people the face of their hearts and which doorway they were to go through next in their lives. The computer was so large that it took up the whole middle intersection where narrow streets converged.

The computer itself looked like a giant thick, brilliant white cloud, but with a distinct form to it. In order to enter and pass through the glory computer each person had to bend down or humble themselves by repenting to remove their sin. Repentance allowed people to fit through the low, narrow doorway. The computer only worked for those who walked through it with a good or pure heart. Those with an unrepentant heart that resisted change would simply walk around in a blind confusion trying to feel their way through the unending maze of life's challenges.

As I walked through the misty door I could feel something like curtains gently brushing against my face. I had to give a little soft push to move through and past the veil like material. My first desire upon entering the computer was to seek Jesus' face. The moment my thoughts turned towards Jesus the veil was removed. Instantly, I was able to lift up my head.

Before me I saw a magnificent ancient door. Above the thick mantel of the door was an engraved sign with the words written "King of Glory" "The Lord Strong and Mighty in Battle." A voice said, "I love you because you have persevered in My Word!" "Behold you have found He who is holy, who is true, who has the key of David, who opens and no one will shut, and who shuts and no one opens. 'I know your deeds so I have put before you an open door which no one can shut, because you have a little power, and have kept My Word, and have not denied My name.'" Upon acknowledging the voice I was given the key of David. This ancient key unlocked the door to my heart and five senses. Each entry became like a golden gateway for the King of Glory to enter into me. All the doors in my body and soul flowed with power and the gates within my mind and spirit were totally open to revelation. I was totally enveloped, transformed and perfected by God's glorious presence.

When I looked again, my hands were unsoiled and my heart was translucent. My soul had been cleansed of all falsehood and deceit. I was washed clean without spot or wrinkle. I felt the blessing of the Lord's righteousness as it came upon me (Psalm 24:4–10). Now the computer began to change and rewrite programs to correct patterns that had not been right in my life. Mountains of opposition were brought low and the valleys of depression were lifted up (Luke 3:4–6) to form a highway of holiness (Isaiah 35). Everything was made new, right and placed in its proper alignment. The righteousness of God empowered me to be able to hold to God's ways. I continued to grow stronger and stronger (Job 17:9). I don't remember coming out of this computer, but I was slowly making my way through, progressing up a spiral staircase step by step.

Behind the outline of this omniscient God computer, I could see coastal fronts with the ocean's water beyond. The coasts were dotted with what looked like a row of huge warehouses or granaries. These kingdom training facilities were going to be used to contain and equip the massive harvest of new believer's souls. Those who successfully graduated from the computer's training programs were transformed to do the greater works and exploits for the end time harvest.

I went to sleep talking to Holy Spirit about John Chapter 15. The Word says, "If you abide in Me and My Words abide in you, you can ask what you will and it will be done for you." The computer represented the glory of Father God, the Holy Spirit's all-knowing presence and the powerful love of Jesus, the Living Word. While I was in the computer, I asked for God's Kingdom to come and for His will to be done in me. I knew it would surely come to pass quickly.

Computer language is a code made up of a google of numbers. Every letter we see and therefore every Word we read in the Bible is also a series of gematria numbers strung together. So, as I pressed my way through this computer, (His Word) my clean heart allowed me to be found in Christ. My faith was activated so that things that were not would begin to be as though they were. Forgetting the past I pressed on until my attitudes were conformed to His. I knew Jesus in the fellowship of His suffering, being conformed to His death; I exited in His resurrection power (Philippians 7:3–16). Now, having taken hold of eternal life, I was ready to fight the good fight of faith. By confessing my testimony in Christ, in the presence of many witnesses, they would see the salvation of the Lord in their lives too (1 Timothy 6:12).

God has visited earth on many occasions in various forms. He daily walked with Adam and Eve in the Garden. He appeared to Abram in dreams. God materialized to His prophets in clouds of glory on mountain tops. He appeared as light, and a burning bush; to Joshua Jesus came as a Theophany or Lord of Host. Jesus came as a baby, walked among men and died on a cruel cross, was buried and resurrected to ascend back to heaven. The Holy Spirit visited mankind on the Day of Pentecost through the sound of a mighty rushing wind and tongues of fire that rested on the heads of the hundred and twenty. That was a foretaste of the powerful visitation God has scheduled for us today. Throughout history we have celebrated the Day of Pentecost with the hope that God would send the fire with a new sound to rest upon His people once again. When believers awaken to the great potential that God has placed within us as the sons of God the whole earth will respond to the manifestations of God's Word spoken through faith filled individuals.

When a spiritual unity is released through the power of love and we arise as one people nothing will be impossible. When each person yields their strength, anointing, and faith a corporate body of Christ will arise as a glory cloud with healing in their wings. The greater works generation will come forth covering the world with unprecedented signs, wonders and miracles. The resurrection of the dead will be common place; no disease will be able to stand in the presence of this mighty God resting upon His purified bride.

The presence of God hovering over the nation of Israel caused them to hear colors and the secret thoughts and intents of hearts, they smelled numbers, tasted sound, and saw voices. Could they have been experiencing what it was like to walk with God in the Garden before man's consciousness fell and was no longer able to tap into the higher spiritual sound waves of revelation knowledge? For a brief moment they were whole again. But, instead of rushing in to experience more of God their sinful state caused them to retreat in fear. How would you respond in a similar encounter?

Chapter 2
Wilderness Preparation

The Holy Spirit led Jesus into the wilderness to be tested and tried in things that were not from His Father, but that were from Satan. The devil tempted Jesus in three areas of worldly yearning: the lust of the flesh, the lust of the eyes and the pride of life, (1 John 2:16). We too will be tested in these same three areas.

These difficult tests demonstrated that Jesus was able to overcome trying situations with His enhanced character and His integrity still intact. The successful completion of these tests allowed Jesus to exit the wilderness carrying the unlimited miracle power of God's love to save a dying world, after having been tempted in the same ways as the world He was sent to reach. Following forty days and nights of fasting Jesus was no doubt in a physically weakened condition when the tempter came to him. Satan wanted Jesus to act independently of His Father and violate the miracle realm by turning stones into bread to satisfy His own physical hunger. Jesus would have acted in disobedience by accessing the supernatural faith realm to do a miracle when His Father was not turning stones to bread. Miracles always defy the natural realm. Jesus set the example by only doing miracles He saw transpiring in the realm of vision. Jesus only did what He saw His Father doing in heaven and that is why He had a 100% success rate.[1]

We learn how to overcome darkness when we walk through the dark night of the soul with the Holy Spirit as our guide to teach, heal and deliver us. "The dark night reveals who we are currently, and when we awaken to a bright new day, Holy Spirit shows us who we can become in Christ." We are children of God's light and bearers of His Glory. We must not get discouraged when we set our hearts to seek more of God. For changes must take place in us before we can see His face. Often in this process there are long barren periods when we do not hear God's voice or sense His presence. Our hope begins to diminish as the light continues to fade until seemingly it goes out, leaving us all alone. At this point, most people give up their faith. They lose hope in the darkest part of the night, right when God was poised and ready to reveal the part of Him we were so desperately seeking.

If our life is totally surrendered to God, and the darkness still persists, we can know that we are going through the refiner's fire. The fire refines our offerings so our lives can be presented in righteousness thus furthering the kingdom. The Lord prunes and disciplines those He loves so they can be more fruitful.

God's hand has always sculpted fiery champions. Saul was blinded when he encountered the face of the living God. Saul had spent a lifetime studying the Word of God. But, it is not merely words that cultivate the soul, it is God Himself. Saul was a brilliant intellectual. He was in an elite class of his own. Saul was discipled by Gamaliel, one of Israel's most respected teachers. As a disciple of Gamaliel, Saul learned to strictly follow man's traditions and adhered to their ways which often conflicted with God's kingdom-ways of heaven. Saul became a zealous persecutor of God's truth; until he was blinded by the light of the Lord's appearing, and was converted on the Road to Damascus.

The light of God blinded Saul on the Road to Damascus and began the preparation process of purifying his heart. Saul was blinded in the natural so, as the Apostle Paul, he could see in the realms of the Spirit. Saul lost his normal sight; but more importantly as Paul, his spiritual eyes were opened to see from God's divine perspective. Paul gained a spiritual insight from his heavenly encounter with God. To have true spiritual vision our spiritual eyes must be opened by the Spirit of God.

The natural must be seen through the eyes of the divine supernatural otherwise it remains commonplace, ordinary and natural. Saul as a natural man did not accept the things of the Spirit of God; for they were foolishness to him. He could not understand them because he lacked wisdom and discernment for the holy is only apprehended by spiritually appraisal. When we finally encounter the Living God face to face, we are then able to spiritually appraise all things. We are all ultimately called to have our minds renewed through spiritual transformation to become members of a supernatural heavenly kingdom. When the spiritual transformation takes place, we are finally able to see to bring forth out of God's treasury things new and old.

After Paul's encounter with a living God; Christ became more real and valuable than anything else on earth. To the true believer God ceases being a principle or ideal and becomes a living reality. God patiently waits to exhibit His grandeur to the humble soul who is pure in heart. The world cries out to know and encounter a living unchangeable God but without repentance they continue to perish for a lack of knowledge. The church maintains its weakened state because we fail to embrace the ways of the Spirit of God and find ourselves in dire want of His powerful presence although we remain planted in God and He is in us.

Spiritual maturity and visionary sight do not happen immediately. Saul did not become God's Apostle Paul overnight. It took a lifelong process of spiritual transformation, and the renewing of his mind to enable him to think from a godly, spiritual perspective. For Saul to become Paul, he had to unlearn of the ways of man, so that he could become a disciple of the kingdom of heaven.

Paul isolated himself in the wilderness for fourteen years. There in seclusion the Holy Spirit corrected Paul's doctrine and trained his spirit to correctly interpret and call to remembrance the truths of things he had learned. Paul was not taught by man. The anointing taught Paul God's ways; he had to unlearn the religious traditions of man that nullified the power of God. Later Paul wrote, "As for you, the anointing which you received from Him abides in you, and you have no need for anyone to teach you; but as His anointing teaches you about all things, and is true and is not a lie, and just as it has taught you, you abide in Him" (1 John 2:27).

Due to the magnitude of sacred revelation Paul received in heavenly places, he was given a spiritual messenger from Satan that buffeted him throughout his years. For Paul his suffering was worth all he lost. To know Christ in the Excellencies of His resurrection power, Paul counted everything else as dung. It is the same for each of us. We each must embrace a spiritual transformation to have our eyes opened to see the face of an invisible God.

We are being taught by the same loving Holy Spirit who intently taught Paul in the desert. The only difference between Paul and us is that we have not totally understood the process or the importance of being drawn away into a single focus to perceive God's wilderness ways. "Now we have received, not the spirit of the world, but the Spirit who is from God, so that we may know the things freely given to us by God, which things we also speak, not in words taught by human wisdom, but in those taught by the Spirit, combining spiritual thoughts with spiritual words" (1 Corinthians 2:12–13).

The Holy Spirit transformed Saul from a religiously blind, persecutor of the real church of Jesus Christ, into a spiritually enlightened Apostle Paul. When Paul finally emerged from his metamorphosis he boldly declared, "I would have you know, brethren, that the gospel which was preached by me is not according to man. For I neither received it from man, nor was I taught it, but I received it through a revelation of Jesus Christ" (Galatians 1:11–12). After Saul's crucifixion process was completed and Christ began to live through the new man, Paul affirmed, "I do all to the glory of God." Paul's life became a constant tribute to the glory of God.

The book of Revelation is the testimony of Jesus Christ not of the anti-christ. Revelation is the lifting of a cover or veil so we can see and access Jesus more clearly. As we retreat to the isle to experience Christ as John the Beloved and Paul did in the wilderness, we will also become mighty instruments, champions of kingdom advancement in the hands of a mighty God.

When we are hidden in the Lord, we are taught to perceive His presence by faith, being touched in our spirit not just in our emotions. Here we learn to be still, develop peace, and patience as we seek God wholeheartedly walking by faith to develop our confident trust in God alone. We renew our minds in wisdom and understanding, waiting upon the Word of the Lord.

We cry out in desperation when we are not able to discern God's presence yet He promises, "I will never leave you or forsake you." God speaks in a still, small voice of whispers so we learn to still ourselves in the darkness of silence to listen in peaceful rest. God teaches us how to restrain our soul (mind, will, emotions) so that our spirit can lead and flourish as we become hungry for God's presence, rest, and peace. "Be still and know that I am God" (Psalm 46:10).

God reveals Himself to us in the desert. We enter the desert full of ourselves, and man's knowledge. God empties us so He can refill us with the seven spirits of His presence, the reverential fear of His wisdom, counsel, knowledge, understand, might and power (Isaiah 11:2).

Our enemy Satan is a liar, destroyer and the diabolical prince of evil darkness. The Almighty Glorious God of light also shrouds Himself in dark clouds yet as we approach God's throne His light brings us to our knees in worship and total surrender so we can walk in the greater light of His power. The God of wonder and radiance bowed the heavens and came down to place darkness under His feet. God made darkness a pavilion around Him. Dark waters surround and thick clouds envelop Him so that we are protected and not consumed by His magnificence.

Often we do not understand the masterful plan God has or comprehend that God is working on our behalf because His ways are so much higher than our ways. But as we hold on to and exercise our faith, looking up to see His face, we gain the courage to press on and yield to God's handiwork, trusting in God to finish that good work which He has begun in us. In surrender, we open our fists and stop fighting the process. We open our hearts to receive His love, for God is doing us good, not evil. He desires to give us the treasures of darkness, and hidden riches of secret places, that we may know that He is the Lord and that He has called each of us by a new name.

When we understand, and come into agreement with the dreams God has created for us, we are propelled into the position we were destined to fill. No one else on earth can live the dream God has inspired for you. Trusting in God, and obediently following His plans, ensures we will reach our destiny on time.

How do you see yourself? How do others view you? Do you know the thoughts that God has towards you? Did you know that God is always thinking positive thoughts about you? God desires to fulfill His divine promises to you. God is always strategically aligning us for success. In order to do this sometimes God has to bring us full circle, back to the beginning, to recall a dream He gave decades ago. He knows the plans of wellbeing He has in mind for us; plans that will give us a new hope for the future. God listens to us when we call on Him. When we pray and seek Him with our whole heart we will find His beautiful face and tender blue eyes that have been gazing upon us all along. When we embrace the dreams God has designed, He is able to exchange the ashes of our pitiful failures for the beauty of His great success.

God shows us who we were, who we are, and who we are created to become, in the dreams He sends. He sees you in a totally different light than you see yourself. People may see you in a limited or narrow way, but God sees you reaching your greatest possible destiny in and through Him. God always views us through His eyes of love. When we agree with the way God sees us, we begin the transformation process. This allows God to accelerate things in our lives. We begin to catch up with God's time table. He is able to restore to us the years that the devourers of failure and missed opportunities have consumed.

God designed the dreams that reside within us to come to light at a particular point in our lives. God strategically releases His dreams within us at a designated time, and then from that moment on, He relates to us as a whole, new, completed person. He no longer communicates to us according to our past or how we were, before the dream imprinted making the needed changes in our spiritual DNA.

Dreams have the power to impart, renew, heal, transform, and reprogram us. If we don't come into the understanding of the dream and correctly interpret it, against the backdrop of God's prescribed script, we can lose valuable time. But, if we understand the message of our dreams, God will accelerate our timeline and increase our measure of blessings.

When we are faithful in the little things, like recording and interpreting our dreams, God trusts us with the grander scales of revelation knowledge. The more we hunger for God, the further we will grow in our ability to taste His goodness. We touch God with our heart and see the internal wonders of His beauty with our eyes. When we passionately love God we delight in the discipline of spiritual pursuits, so God can trust us with great riches in both the natural and spiritual realms.

Never allow complacency to take root or spiritual growth will become stagnant. Spiritual hunger must take precedent over everything else or the simplicity of Christ will not manifest in that person's dreams. God reveals Himself to babes, those with a childlike faith, but He hides Himself from the wise in thick darkness. When we have God dwelling within us, we have the source of all there is to have and know. When we have God, we have nothing to lose, even if we lost everything.

Once understanding comes in a specific area of our lives, God continues to build upon that level of understanding until we are able to grasp a higher or fuller knowledge of His ways. God relates to us, as if we have already become the amazing person He designed us to be from the beginning. The old person no longer exists; all things have become new in Christ. This is why it is imperative that we continue to focus on and call to remembrance the mighty things God has spoken to us in His Word and through our dreams.

Grace and peace are multiplied to us when our knowledge of His ways and plans for our lives become preeminent. Seeing the plans and purposes God has reserved for our success in dreams allows us to achieve them. God's divine plans are written on the tablets of our heart. As we study to show ourselves approved, as a friend of God, His training and equipping process allows us to progress and step into our destiny.

Every increase or advancement in life involves a step-by-step process. God's patience woos and draws us to Himself by the touch of the Holy Spirit's breath. We hear and feel the Spirit's call and respond to His gentle contact and prompting. We see the plan of salvation and accept it as a gift. Now the Holy Spirit has activated all five of our spiritual senses. We smell His presence arrive, feel His touch, hear His voice, taste that He is good, and we see His plan for our lives in Christ. We have to hear His voice in the Word to have faith; we have to see Him, to be like Him. We need to understand His plan to embrace it in its fullness. We must believe that God rewards those who diligently seek His face and do His will. God's presence is a sweet smelling savor.

God is within us. This is the generation of God-seekers who search for Him day and night. We continually seek God's face and with God's help we will find Him. We study God's Word to train our spiritual and natural gifts to become the person God has destined us to become. When our training process is mature, because it never ends, we become His witnesses proclaiming His greatness, interpreting His spiritual expressions, boldly demonstrating His power with signs, wonders and miracles following.

Our spiritual journey is not one of the minds, but one of the hearts felt love. Let us seek God through the dreams of the night and the trances of thought that entertain, when our blinded eyes are finally given visionary sight that is emboldened by His grace. Let the Holy Spirit's whispers of wisdom come to the prudent. Let the deaf ears hear and encourage our mouths to speak of His grace.

When we seek God's face, we should expect to gain understanding of the mysteries received in the treasures of darkness. Spiritual riches are hidden in dreams, in the secret place of His eternal presence. Those who seek the Lord understand all things. He who trusts in the Lord will prosper and be exalted. And those who know Your name will put their trust in You; for You, Lord, have not forsaken those who seek You (Psalm 9:10).

God's ways are past finding out. God's love is eternal, it has no beginning or end, no limit, for His love is incomprehensibly vast. God's perfect love casts fear out of His beloved. Love wills a person good and everlasting welfare, never harm or evil. Love gives freely to the object of its affection holding no record of wrong. We are the friends of a loving God who laid down His life for us. Herein is love that while we were sinners and enemies of God He sent His only Son Jesus, to die for humanity.

God's favor rests upon those who allow Him to correctly position them to reach their greatest potential. Success comes when we expect success. When our hope is centered on Christ our expectations will draw God's wisdom, goodness and favor, to lead and guide us to become successful. When we are correctly positioned, we will live and move and have our being in God. Success comes from God, cycles through Him, and flows like a circuit back to Him. The Father is continually emptying Himself into Jesus. The Holy Spirit then empowers Jesus to empty Himself back into the Father so the cycle of giving and sharing love never ends.

When we discover the mind of God, He becomes the wise counselor to us. Dreams issue an invitation that allows us to see ourselves the way God sees us both now, in the future, and for all eternity. Our identity in God is bigger and better than the way we see ourselves today. True knowledge and authority come through experiencing the Living Word, Jesus, in our lives.

Before we were created God skillfully crafted all of our days. He nestled dreams and visions deep within our soul before He created time. God alone knows the beginning from the end. He existed before time began, and God will exist after the final grain of sand slips through the neck of time's hourglass.

Chapter 3
Everyone Dreams

Dreams are our subconscious inner man at work revealing our true nature. Dreams have many emotional, physical, and spiritual benefits. Similar to the powers of our imagination, dreaming is a universal human phenomenon uniting people across barriers of age, gender, racial background, social differences, and historical circumstances. Dreams bring access to spiritual messages about blessing, and visions bring insight into God's plans. Dreams bring us vision and guidance in everyday life and circumstances. Dreams free our minds, provide clarity, dispel confusion, and enable us to function with mental lucidity during the day. Dreams release accumulated tension and fear, and they bring release from built up stress by providing a vacation for our minds.

Dreams answer questions, and bring wisdom to solve difficult problems. They make us aware of how to break bad, perplexing habits, and how to remove hindrances, or obstacles that are keeping us from reaching destiny. Dreams unleash us into creativity, and inventiveness. They make us more open, flexible, and attuned to our God-given abilities.

Dreams have the ability to take us out of the natural realms of time. They can move us back into the past, help us to deal with the present, or launch us into the future. The past is history, so it can not hold us; the future is a mystery, so we must seek God for understanding; and the present is the gift God has given for us to enjoy. A dream aligns us with the present moment while exposing us to future realities and possibilities.

When we look into a dream, we are gazing at a mirrored reflection of the natural or subconscious image of ourselves. Just like in a mirror, by looking into our dream life we can see qualities of ourselves represented by characters or symbols in the dream. Spiritually speaking, we are known fully and completely by a loving Creator. Now we see but a poor reflection, as in a mirror; then we shall see face to face. Now I know in part; then I shall know fully, even as I am fully known (1 Corinthians 13:12 NIV).

We are destined to reflect God's character and image when we come to know His different dimensions. The closer we draw to the Creator, the more of His light we absorb. His brightness illuminates and changes us so that we can finally see ourselves clearly. We are beings of light because God our Creator is the Father of Light. We are called to live a life where nothing is hidden in darkness, but where everything is exposed to His light. Things that are concealed in darkness will detract from our potential. Dreams bring light to our lives by dispelling the darkness, so we do not stumble or fall.

God transforms us through the images He projects upon the screens of our hearts. He speaks tender, life-giving, creative words. When we obediently embrace these faith filled messages, positive changes take place. If we ignore God's messages of love, tragically, we remain the same. People, who refuse to change, stagnate and remain unaffected. They forget who they are and who divine intervention called them to become. When we stop the process of metamorphosis, we risk never realizing our destiny.

Dreams mirror the image of the soul by reflecting our inner condition. They display what will become apparent if positive adjustments take place. But, tragically, they also reveal what will transpire if no alteration or negative changes take place in us.

Prayer Preparation for Sleep

Prayer is a powerful tool to prepare for sleep. I anoint myself every night with my fragrant 'Dream Encounter' anointing oil before going to bed. The beautiful clean scent creates a serene aromatic atmosphere of peace. It is important to honor God for His love and great mercy by thanking Him for who He is, and for always watching over our lives. Ask God to demonstrate His plans and purposes in the dreams of the night. A visionary experience during the dreams of the night makes it easy to follow God's guidance. When we submit to Holy Spirit's supervision, we will see His power to save us established. Prayer is able to remove sin, stress and fear, replacing them with a confidence in God and a serene dream that assures us that everything is going to be fine. Through repentance and rest we are saved; in quietly trusting God, we are strengthened.

Confession is good for the soul because it sets us free. It removes the power of darkness and releases light to spring forth. Confessing our fears to God and bringing them to the light breaks chains of bondage. If we will ask the Holy Spirit to show us the wisdom of God's ancient paths or ways, He will. We are called to walk in prosperity and follow in the good ways. We will stand and be strengthened by observing the ways of God. When we walk in the paths of purity with a clean heart, we will find rest for our souls. "Is not your fear of God your confidence and the integrity of your ways your hope (Job 4:6)?" By placing our confidence in God, and not in our own abilities, sleep is insured.

Dear Jesus,

Thank You for Your continual watchful presence in my life. Let my sleep be sweet and refreshing to revitalize my body. Forgive me for the wrongs I committed today in thought, word or deed and remove them far from me. I ask You to visit me. Design dreams that will give me the wisdom I need to solve my problems, show me the way to go. Speak to me through the visions of the night. Station Your angels to waken me at specific times to help me gain clarity and understanding of my dreams by correlating the chapter and verses of Scriptures with my waking times or the date of my dream. Amen

Stress

When people are under the pressure of stress or fear, they often resort to abusing drugs, alcohol, or food to try and alleviate their pain and fears. This will result in less, –or a poorer quality of sleep, thus fewer dreams. People who are in the process of breaking a smoking habit or a cigarette addiction tend to have longer and more extreme dreams. The dreams that arise out of a drug or alcohol induced sleep are often forgotten, fragmented or tormenting in nature. The story they tell doesn't bring hope or relief, but magnifies the negative, destructive fears and dreadful feelings that produce more stress and anxiety.

Stress does not come from outside forces, but from within the internal belief system of a person. Stress comes from our fearful responses to negative pressures. Stress doesn't appear because you are the topic of gossip, accusation, or someone scheming to cause your downfall or demise. Stress comes because you have allowed the fear of the unknown: What may or may not happen; fear of what is being said, or done to take root in your heart. You have believed the veiled threats of the enemy more than you believe that God is able to defend, deliver, and promote you past the enemy's ability to touch you. King David said, "Because of the voice of the enemy, because of the pressure of the wicked; for they bring down trouble upon me and in anger they bear a grudge against me. My heart is in anguish within me, and the terrors of death have fallen upon me. Fear and trembling come upon me, and horror has overwhelmed me." (Psalms 55:3–5)

Dreams show us the ways of God's wisdom. Dreams show us the way of escape and how to overcome. Dreams provide the needed answers to slay the Jabberwockies that ghoulishly loom over us as they strike from the shadows of fear.

Fear can stop us cold in our tracks if we allow it to paralyze our forward momentum. Fear, or anxiety dreams, can spring up when we are walking down a new path, or opening a door we have never been through before. Any major life change can ignite fear dreams. Getting engaged, married, having a baby, becoming a mother or father, going off to college, taking the bar exam or starting a new career, or preparing a speech to present in public, can trigger nightmares. It is important to confront the proverbial fears of "What if I fail?" instead of avoiding them. If we don't deal with our fear of failure, our worries will continue to take us down the horrible "what if" avenue of no return.

Sometimes our belief systems or spiritual upbringing conflicts with our objective feelings, wants, desires or physical urges. We find ourselves in a tug of war battling between what we know is right but wanting to do what is wrong or expedient for the moment. It is always important to count the cost before moving forward on the wrong path of expediency. Never sacrifice your future success on the altar of the immediate.

Gratification always comes with a price. When you are unable to move, walk or run in your dream, ask yourself if you are sinking your future in the quicksand of compromise, instead of building your future on the firm foundation of character and integrity. Your spirit knows the right path to take to succeed in life. Don't allow your soul, the mind, will or emotions, to lead when there are important life changing decisions to make. Allow your conscience to lead after a time of spiritual communion and prayer. Wisdom will come and guide you to the appropriate answer. The paralysis will lift and you will once again run the race to win. Success is assured when the spirit of man follows the leading of the Holy Spirit. When our decisions are not led by the peace of the Holy Spirit, we experience stress.

I was lecturing at a business meeting on how to handle stress in today's society. As an example I picked up a water glass from one of the tables. The audience expected me to poise the question "half empty or half full?" But, instead I lifted the glass up with ease and began carrying it around the room. I inquired, "How much does this glass of water weigh?" The audiences giggled and their answers ranged from 6oz. to 12oz.

I replied with a smile "The weight is really irrelevant. What really matters is how long I continue to hold the glass of water. If I hold it for a moment or two, just a few minutes, there is no problem. If I continue to hold it for the rest of the lecture my arm may start to ache. If I hold it for the rest of the night without placing it down my arm will feel numb and paralyzed. In each instance the weight of the glass has not changed but the length of time I have entertained it has increased. The longer I carry the glass the heavier it appears to become and the more it affects me physically. The stresses and worries of life are like this glass of water. If we casually think about them for a moment nothing happens. But if we start to focus on them and carry them with us everywhere we go they begin to weigh us down. If we carry them in front of us all the time they will hurt us. We will begin to feel paralyzed. If we allow our troubles and stress to overwhelm us we are then powerless of doing anything. It is important to cast our stresses and cares on Jesus daily; let go of them, put them down. Once you have placed your troubles on Jesus, pray, then go to sleep in peace and don't pick them back up in the morning."

Do you suffer from stress, fear, or anxiety? Do you have the fear of man? Do you fear failure or rejection? There are multiplied thousands of different forms of fear but none of them are from God. The presence of God comes to give abundant life, joy in its fullness, peace, and rest. "Come to me all of you who are tired from the heavy burden you have been forced to carry. I will give you rest. Accept My teaching. Learn from Me. I am gentle and humble in spirit. And you will be able to get some rest. Yes, the teaching that I ask you to accept is easy. The load I give you to carry is light." (Matthew 11:28–30)

God promises to give His beloved sleep. The only person we should fear is God. He alone can destroy both the body and the soul in hell. He is the Holy One who created life and lovingly holds the whole world in the palm of His magnificent hands. Don't be afraid of people. They can only kill your physical body, not your soul.

Chapter 4 Dream Wisdom & the Power to Solve Problems

God uses dreams to remove stress and to instruct us in wisdom. Wisdom is the ability to recognize opportunities that are generated when an obstacle or difficulty presents itself. A problem is an invitation to obtain stature and reward. We are rewarded with honor, riches, and long life when we walk in humility. The humble have learned the key to success is seeking the Lord. They make right choices and follow godly principles in life.

Destiny is realized when we develop a history of overcoming obstacles. A history of solving the problems of the past leads to future promotions. When a big problem is knocking at your door, answer it; because a promotion is on the horizon.

To solve a problem one must first admit they have a problem that they cannot solve on their own. Then, show some initiative by asking God for His help and wisdom. The presence of problems can ignite positive changes. Problems position us to remove negative situations and relationships. Tribulations attract people with kindred spirits that will lift you up and carry you up the steep steps of promotion. When you pray, God will send the people you need to create your next platform. New people will bring fresh knowledge, wisdom and the needed skill sets. These relational building currencies are invaluable treasures.

Make a decision to change the way you think about and respond to problems. Respond by praying and seeking God's counsel. Answer difficult people in grace and love. Allow problems to change your heart, mind and negative habits. Take authority over negative thought patterns; let the Word of God renew your mind.

God provides by giving us the words of wisdom when we ask Him. Prayer demonstrates a greater measure of trust in and submission to God.

The humble, gentle person has an advantage because they trust God to defend them. Wisdom and humility act in response to God's leading but does not react to people who try to provoke or persecute. Allow God to intervene and do not defend yourself to others. Let your enemies work for and benefit you by pointing out your shortcomings or weaknesses; then make the necessary changes to improve yourself. Don't preserve yourself; let the Advocate Jesus either defend or change you. The principal purpose of wisdom is to develop the ability to determine who should be honored more than others. Everyone is created in God's image; so everyone, even the lowliest of persons, is deserving of a measure of honor.

God's wisdom comes to us in dreams to give us the power to become a clarion voice or whatever we need to become in every circumstance. God's wisdom enables us to solve problems and every enigma. The Word of God, which is the living wisdom of God in written form, comes to us in picture images through the dreams of the night. God created and rules the universe with His powerful Word. Wisdom is the ability to know the difference between right and wrong, when to bow and when to take a stand. Your ability to solve the problems in life lies in your ability to hear God's voice and understand God's Word. Your knowledge of and your ability to correctly apply God's Word determines your impact, measure of influence and significance.

Experts are paid large sums of money because they are able to solve difficult, unique problems. Anyone can solve a small problem but the solution brings very little recognition or gratitude. Little bitty problems produce little bitty muscles of faith; but the person who is able to correctly discern God's symbolic dream or spiritual language will be given a great problem solving advantage over others. Kings and Presidents will seek out and befriend the dream seer and interpreter while promoting them in the court of their counsel.

David was a lowly shepherd boy when he recognized an opportunity to gain the audience to converse with King Saul. David became a valiant warrior when he delivered Israel from the base insults of the giant Goliath. David moved from the lonely pastures to the spacious, palatial palace. A lowly pauper married a beautiful princess. David emerged from the shadows of the king, as a king himself. Wisdom is the ability to recognize the opportunities that are generated when a giant obstacle, mystery or difficulty presents itself. We have been given the opportunity to converse with the King of Kings through dreams, visions and prayer on a daily basis. What a great honor and opportunity. When we spend quality time with the King we will become kingly, like Him.

Even the blind man saw opportunity and had enough wisdom to 'cry out' when Jesus was passing by. As well, a common criminal, condemned and hanging on a cross, discerned that there was something divinely different about Jesus. He cried out, "Lord, remember me when you come into Your kingdom!"

Peter saw a vision of a sheet full of creatures being let down; then a voice spoke to him twice. His thinking had to be renewed to receive the call of God on his life before he could effectively touch the Gentiles. "Peter went up on the housetop about the sixth hour to pray. But he became hungry and was desiring to eat; but while they were making preparations, he fell into a trance; and he saw the sky opened up, and an object like a great sheet coming down, lowered by four corners to the ground, and there were in it all kinds of four-footed animals and crawling creatures of the earth and birds of the air. A voice came to him, "Get up, Peter, kill and eat!" But Peter said, "By no means, Lord, for I have never eaten anything unholy and unclean." Again a voice came to him a second time, "What God has cleansed, no longer consider unholy." (Acts 10:9–15)

The words of God's statutes and judgments enable us to live victorious lives so we can become all God has dreamed of us becoming.

Chapter 5
Embraced by a Living God

Holy Spirit embraces and hovers over mankind while we sleep. He imparts vision and recalls dreams that beckon us to pursue Him with all of our hearts. Paul prays, in (Ephesians 1:17–19), that believers may be enlightened in our understanding in order to have the riches of His glorious power manifested in our lives. Every believer must be led by the Spirit of wisdom and revelation to comprehend the Father's heart. God expands our knowledge, revelation and relationship with Him in our daily lives through experiencing His touch and activity. When we adhere to His heavenly perspectives it has entrance into the world. God opens our blinded eyes to see life the way He sees our existence. God's vision and higher ways enables us to see our destiny and the world events around us from His positive vantage point. God alone has all the answers for which we search.

Spiritual understanding or enlightenment is different than natural wisdom because it has always been within God. The presence of God comes through the Holy Spirit resting upon our five natural senses. He emboldens our natural vision, hearing, touch, taste, and smell for us to know how the Spirit realm operates. Holy Spirit attracts us to Jesus so we can choose salvation. After salvation, Jesus, the Lover and perfecter of our soul, comes in different measures as we commune with Him daily. God reveals Himself to us through increased measures of His Holy Spirit presence and power.

Spiritual wisdom empowers us to know what the future holds. In contrast, spiritual knowledge enables us to replicate past experiences (both victorious accomplishments and heart breaking disappointments) through the eyes of God. Applying godly wisdom to past failures resets a new course that directs us to apprehend God's grace for success and prosperity. True success only comes through the exercise of aggressive faith.

The Holy Spirit inspires our nights with hopeful dreams, colorful visions and inspiring visitations of many and varied kinds. God carries us through a spiritual preparation process in our dreams to ready us to see our potential to accomplish great adventures. We experience new opportunities in the night seasons so that we will be familiar with it in broad daylight. (1 John 3:2–3) states that as children of God, we will be able to see things that have not yet been made known, and as we see God in our dreams and visions, we will be like Him.

What we place our focus upon, embrace or study we empower. Whatever we empower becomes a part of our lives. We are converted into what we sanction in our lives. To enact this practice into our lives we are admonished to magnify the Lord. When we magnify God we do not make Him bigger for He is already the All in All. But, we see Him as larger than life; and we are then drawn into the safety of His presence. When God's Word is amplified in our hearing, it draws the Holy Spirit and His angels into our situations. When the angelic realm hears His anointed Word going forth from our mouths, they are released to perform His word on our behalf. It is God's overshadowing presence, manifested through His anointed Word and the Holy Spirit, which changes us from one level of understanding, glory and revelation to another.

We must be totally dependent upon the Holy Spirit for understanding, interpretation and application of the revelation that God has planted within us. All interpretations belong to the Holy Spirit. Our spirit resonates with the creative Words God speaks. God is in Himself everything supreme. Nothing is above or beyond God. He graciously honored man above all the heavenly beings when He created us in His image. From that moment on, the dreams we have are daily recreating us into the image of God; thus we become that which He declared. We echo the sound of His voice and mirror the light of our Creator. When we are connected to Christ, the brightness of God's glory, we become what He has destined for us to be, from before the foundation of the earth. Man exists to give glory to God. The living Word of God consists in spiritual power that grants eternal life. God created and sustains all living beings in heaven and on earth. No unconscious life, conscious human life or self-sufficient angelic being exists separate from God.

The voice of God's wisdom echo's in our dreams throughout creation, "Be at rest in your silence, wait on Me and know that I am God!" Those whose ears are constantly tuned to the present words of heaven's clarion call receive redemptive revelation, astute intelligence; and they see clever inventions, inspired ideas and gain ingenious truths. Let me listen always to the sound of Your voice playing gently upon the strings of my heart. May the melodies of Your Words be music that surrounds me to drown out the constant barrage of noise that assaults my mind. Let my prayer be like that of the boy Samuel, "Speak Lord for your servant listens." We must continue to look unto Jesus the creator and finisher of our faith.

When we accept delivery of God's dream letters of love, He releases the strategic power to change every life event into something wonderful. The Holy Spirit turns negative happenings to our advantage and improvement. Dreams enable us to glance into the imperceptible realms of wisdom, counsel, knowledge and might. The Holy Spirit enables us to accomplish the eternal designs that are clearly chosen for our life. Dreams publicize the great potential and vastness of our future. Dreams heal the pain of the past by removing the sting of failures we would otherwise haul with us through life. Dreams empower us to live each day to its fullest.

Dreams are formed in a person's subconscious mind. They are based on the imagery and secret symbolic language that are exclusive and strategic to that person's particular life and destiny. Dreams emulate that which was embossed on the soul - before time began - when we were still hidden in God's loins. Before time began, each soul (as mere beings of light) was called before the council chambers of God, who is the Father of Light. There each person agreed to the timing of their birth, gender, and nationality. They discussed their tests, trials, triumphs, success and failures to be experienced in life. Once an agreement was made and life was chosen we were extracted from eternity and inserted into the restraint of time. The essence of our being was placed into our mother's womb, and given a natural body. The waiting was over. We stepped out of a limitless eternity into the constraints of time, confined to journey through life in a three dimensional state. Our past, present and future have already been experienced in God, yet they are still becoming reality every day of our lives. The mind's eye is always penetrating the barriers of understanding to learn who we were and into whom we are destined to be renewed.

The mind's eye is the human ability for visual discernment, imagination, visualization, and memory. There is no new revelation under the sun. What is now; has always been, and will always be in God. Our dreams enable us to tap into the grand plan of God for our individual lives. Revelation and dreams arise out of our soul when our spirit connects to, is renewed by, tuned in, and submitted to, the leading of the Holy Spirit.

When creativity comes, it feels as if it is a new, fresh idea, but it has always been within us percolating, waiting for the fullness of time to emerge. In other words, the mind's eye is one's ability to see and create things with the powers of thought.

The mind's eye is able to glance back into the past, before time existed, behold the now, or gaze into the new dimensions of the future.

Dreams enable us to see the plans and purposes God had for us before we entered into this earthly realm of existence. All of our days were numbered and ordered before we were born. Part of our spiritual journey is learning how to enter into the divine scripts of success that have already been written for each of us.

Many dreams are symbolic mysteries that require God's guidance to uncover their hidden meanings. God intends that we know His ways. God desires us to recognize the way He moves and become familiar with Him, through prayer and the process of discovering the veiled meaning of our dreams. These mysterious scripts are encoded with symbolism. The reverential fear of the Lord leads us to apprehend the Spirit of Truth, Wisdom, Counsel, Revelation Knowledge, Might and Understanding which are necessary to accurately direct us in the practice of gaining access or comprehending the meanings of our godly imaginations and visionary symbols.

Dreams bring the revelation of who we are to become in Christ once our spirit is awakened, born again, and then enlightened by the Holy Spirit. This revelation enables each believer to work together as a unit, while keeping our individuality at the same time. We each have a component and diverse function that is displayed through the corporate body of Christ in the progression of life.

If we are open to God, He can access our image center through the medium of the Holy Spirit. The Holy Spirit will grant us dreams in the night, or streams of contemplation during the day, to bring revelation and direct guidance to our lives. These spiritual streams overflow us with foresight, open our eyes to see, and renew our minds by washing away harmful thought patterns that limit our intellectual processes. Dreams awaken our mind's vision to the unlimited possibilities that await us. Nothing is impossible when we attach ourselves to the power of God's love. We are created in God's image. Therefore, we possess the same power to create with our visual images and words. The dreams we envision grant us agreement with the creative realm to eradicate any obstacle that would constrain us to mediocrity.

The world of dream revelation enables us to peer into the otherwise hidden spiritual past, present, or future dimensions. The spiritual depths we are able to see depends on our own belief system, knowledge, faith level and confidence in God's ability to reveal Himself in our current life environment and circumstances. Dreams come to give us peace beyond our ability to understand. They communicate obscure truths and the ambiguous information that our conscious minds overlooked or could not identify during our waking hours. Once we are able to synchronize our subconscious with our conscious limitations, barriers are removed and our potential is realized.

A dream comes to release revelation (whether natural or spiritual) when our body is at rest. Sometimes the only way God can communicate within us, is when our soul is settled enough for Him to speak peace deep into our spirit man.

A dream is like a photograph of something we are able to relate to in movie form. Ecclesiastes 5:3 tells us that a dream comes when there are many concerns, activities or business. Dreams can either be a subconscious response to the circumstances of our lives or the Holy Spirit communicating His plans, ways and purposes to us. Dreams enable us to tap into the superior ways of the Divine Spirit. Precognitive or visionary dreams often reveal the obscure future, making it profoundly clear. Predictive dreams are filled with revelation that causes the dreamer to make the correct decisions to align themselves for a successful future. Our dream life is like a thoroughfare on which communication is carried through the soul to the visualization of the mind's eye to the spirit.

Chapter 6
Faith Makes Dreams Come True

God created the spiritual principle of conceiving revelation, beholding and then by faith conforming to what is seen. To reach the full potential of our God-given destiny the Lord must always be foremost in our eyes. It is important to stay focused on Jesus the goal; and on the destiny designs and purposes that He has set before us. We must see ourselves as God sees us.

Faith is a gift of God that comes by hearing the Word of God. Faith is an indispensible necessity that makes it possible to please God by simply looking upon His countenance for life. The heart of faith looks to God, believing for Him to open up the recesses of impossibilities making everything promised or dreamed possible for the weakest when they are resting in God's hands. Without faith the eyes of the heart are clouded with no spiritual vision or ability to approach God to find forgiveness, healing and eternal life. Faith is empowered by believing that creating the impossible is possible. Faith is found in the power of the spirit to believe that what is hoped for will be created and then drawn into existence in the natural tangible realms of manifestation. Faith is not exercising the force of the mind over matter, or even believing one can control matter, but it is the divine supernatural ability to create substance out of the invisible, imperceptible realm.

We look upon the beautiful face of the Holy Spirit and believe in an invisible God. I sought the Lord for answers. He listened and heard my inward cry of desperation. I meditated upon His Word to focus my gaze and He brought clarity. He communed with me and I beheld Him in the Spirit. He became my Helper and Comforter. I lifted my unveiled eyes unto God who dwells in heaven and

He found His resting place in my heart. My eyes waited upon the Lord until His mercy came and met me in my place of need. He removed the scales from my eyes, now I see His splendor. God delivered me from all my fears and now I am satisfied.

The precious gift of faith enables us to look to God with expectant eyes. Because we believe His Word we can boldly approach God with love and trust in our hearts. In our desperation we seek the face of the Lord. We call out and reveal our heart felt feelings. As we look to Him we grow radiant in His presence. God answers us rescuing us from all of our fears. Our eyes wait upon the Lord until He has mercy on us. The heavenly power the Lord experienced on earth was because He always kept a focused gaze upon the actions of His Father.

Those whose faith continually looks to the Lord will be accepted, enlightened and never be put to shame. As we gaze upon Jesus, we will be transformed and given the power to complete our destiny; that which God has determined for us to accomplish in life. The all-seeing, watchful eyes of the Lord look down from heaven, they move to and fro throughout the whole earth searching for people who are faithful. When the Beloved finds the eyes of the faithful gazing back at Him, totally focused, believing, and expectantly waiting for His wisdom and not looking at themselves or their situations, He makes them strong. God physically demonstrates His powerful support of those whose humble hearts are completely committed. He tunes our hearts so they beat in one accord in harmony with heavens syncopated rhythm.

If we are serious about living a new resurrected life that is full of glory we must seek the reality of things that are above the natural by pursuing the heavenly realms where Christ presides. Jesus is currently seated at the right hand of God so we must set our minds on things that are above and not on earthly things. Believers have been crucified and resurrected into glory with Jesus. Our lives are now hidden in Christ who is within God the Father. Christ, although invisible to spectators, or those who have not yet met Him, is for the Believer life itself. So every time Jesus appears to earthen vessels in our dreams, manifesting Himself through our lives or circumstances we see Him from His higher perspective. We appear with Jesus by operating in faith and the glory He provides for us to do the greater works. When Jesus returns to earth from His heavenly throne will He find us operating in faith?

Faith is the fundamental fact that forms a firm foundation for everything's existence. By placing our trust in God, life becomes worth living. By faith we understand that the whole universe was framed by the Words spoken by God. Faith is what makes real the things we hope for. What is seen was not made out of things that are visible. Faith is the tangible proof of what we cannot currently see. People who live their lives by commanding God's Word to create things through faith are pleasing to God because they are imitating God's actions. Faith helps us understand that God created the whole world and the universe by His command. Great and small acts of faith distinguish Believer's from the crowd.

God is our eternal dwelling place when we are attuned to the voice of the Holy Spirit. Higher understanding surrounds us when our eyes are fixed upon God. Faith enables us to focus outwardly on seeking God instead of fixing our eyes upon ourselves inwardly. We can see God's hand working in every circumstance when our heart is full of love. The Word of God is near you; even the Word of faith within your mouth.

God's loving nature, His creative life giving, spiritual Words, and His symbolic picture language enables us to interpret dreams according to His desires; not according to what man says or what we believe about ourselves. Each heart must learn to interpret a heavenly language as the Spirit instructs and then willfully obey. God has a divine dream plan for each one of us to fulfill. When we are each tuned to God we begin to harmonize with His presence and true unity is formed.

Dreams make it possible for us to reach our destiny. Just like our individual DNA has a unique signature and song, God's heavenly plans, strategies, and blueprints were individually written on the tablets of our heart before time began. It is the Holy Spirit who gives value to us and without the Spirit nothing has lasting value. God places a desire within the heart to know Him. Our spiritual eyes gaze upon the beauty of the Lord exalting Him over all, while our outward man watches the world parade by.

God's holy light ignited His love within those who worship Him in Spirit and truth. The Spirit of truth, compassion and revelation reveals God to us. The more we understand His ways of communication and His nature, the more we fall in love with Him. The more we love God, the more we can love ourselves and others. God's love brings a new divine viewpoint, a different psychology and power is formed within us.

God brings His grand purposes and destiny to our lives through the plans He has for us to succeed. He imparts the power of His spiritual realm, so as ambassadors, we can transfer His spiritual realms to this natural realm. Dreams are one way that God chooses to communicate what He sees in us. Dreams give us the necessary keys to unlock the doors of great grace. Dreams empower us to break out of the restraints of this world, relate to God and bring His manifest kingdom into existence. When we honor God in His preeminence He will honor us with

His presence.

Dreams are a symbolic picture language. Because pictures are easily imprinted on our soul we can recall images. God speaks in a mysterious language of signs, symbols, puns and riddles through dreams. God lovingly speaks to who we are presently and reveals what we can become, rather than emphasizing negatives.

We live in both a physical, natural world that is subject to the limitations of the flesh, and the superior spiritual world where we possess heavenly citizenship, and enjoy intimacy with God. We are not called to walk a tightrope between these two spheres but to live at peace in both realms simultaneously. The dreams we have connect us to both worlds at the same time. Dreams allow us to see what will take place in the future so we can align our lives for success.

Jesus was not divided in His heavenly and earthly existences because He lived His life in full view of His Father's presence. Jesus did all to the glory of God. The hour comes and now is, when the true worshippers shall worship God in Spirit and in truth; for the Father seeks such people to worship Him. God is a Spirit so those who worship Him must learn to do so in Spirit and in truth. For example, God does not cause our sickness and disease; He brings healing and deliverance. God has an infinite ability to restore our health. God does not bring poverty or lack; He promotes wealth, prosperity and abundance. God is the God of more than enough. God does not articulate our failures or mistakes; He announces a plan for our success. God does not exploit the past; He speaks to the now and to a hopeful future. God speaks the language of love and hope to encourage our great success. God's love is without measure it is boundless because it is the essence of His nature. Paul took up this same cry for liberty when he announced all meats to be clean and every day to be holy, all places equally sacred and every act acceptable to God. Prophets, mystics and reformers have fought and will continue to fight to keep us free from the bondage of religious rules and obligations of spiritual slavery.

No one likes to be kept in the dark, guessing whether we have pleased God or not. That is why God carries us into the brightness of His eternal light through our dreams and visions. In the realm of vision God announces the wonderful plans He has for our future. He published His divine dream plans for man in the Bible. God also wrote His dream script upon the tablets of our hearts before time began.

When we capture a picture of light and God's merciful goodness for our lives in the midst of the dark place of our existence, we have 'vision.' Vision produces a hope that is exclusively centered in Christ. Hope enables us to embrace change. Change releases destiny. Destiny drives us out of the now and propels us into a bright future. Once we catch a glimpse of who we are in the future, the doors are opened for us to bring the future into the reality of today. God is able to accelerate wellbeing in our lives through dreams and visions. The more of God we can see and believe, the more like Him we can become. We must see it, write it, say it, pray and decree it, to believe it, and finally to be it! Your dream has to be seeable before it's believable. It has to be believable before it's achievable.

Faith and Visualization

Success comes not only through years of experience, education, talent and hard work; it comes through prayer agreeing with God's purposes and plans for your life. These plans are explored in the deep recesses of your thoughts through visualization in the mind's eye. Please hear me when I say, "Your imagination is not evil; it is what makes you uniquely you." The dreams God sends help you to discover the precious treasures that are buried deep within your subconscious. The Holy Spirit blows on a specific dream segment when the time is right; causing that dimension to surface. When you discover the wonders God has sealed within your being destiny is born.

To achieve your dreams you must record them; designing a sure plan by building a strong frame or support structure. Everyday you must keep moving forward, walking one step at a time, by doing something positive you move closer to accomplishing your God given dreams and goals. To achieve your dreams or aspirations you must first organize all the processes that will be required, listing them in a rational sequence of succession. Every step you take in life gives you another chance to change and improve the life you live.

Where do you want to go in life? What do you want to accomplish? Did you know that if you are able to see what you want, you will get what you see? Dreams draw a picture that allows us to travel on a prescribed path to reach our destiny. The fulfillment of life's dreams is similar to the process of arranging the pieces of the puzzle in a straight line until we know which ones come first and which one will be last. As we make the continued effort to take one small piece of the puzzle or single baby step at a time, this consistent movement will help us keep walking into our future on a planned timeline.

Instead of always pressing forward, occasionally, look backward to commemorate your advancements then celebrate how far you have come by thinking those who helped you succeed. If you get stuck, work backwards until you find the answer or what has caused you to falter. Do not postpone actions or procrastinate when it is in your power to advance. Keep leaning in, be methodical and systematic, exercising steady movement that is deliberate and consistent. Stop vacillating, know where you are going, just like you determine your destination before you start a trip, make up your mind that you are going to succeed and with God's help you will.

Dreams are God's stepping stones that lead to change. The Apostle James told us that if we need wisdom we should ask God because He is generous and giving. But if we ask God we should believe and not doubt what He tells us. The person who doubts is like a wave on the sea that is blown about by the wind. People who think two things at the same time are double-minded thus unstable in all their ways. They do not have the faith to receive from the Lord; so they cannot decide what to do, so they end up doing nothing. They remain adrift and never achieve their life purpose. If you do not know what you want, you will not achieve it! If you have not written down your dreams and visions with their interpretations, you will not succeed. In order to leave one place, you need to know where you are going before you will be able to discern if you have arrived. Visualization is an internal GPS to help you determine where you are currently and then decide where you want to be in the future.

Are you serious about the dreams you have been given? Greatness is not calculated in the miles we travel or in the amount of money or material possessions we have accumulated but in a heart that is full of love. Prominence arises amongst the thousands of creative thoughts we sort through everyday carefully selecting the golden ones to plant, water and develop.

Creative thinking will bring us from thoughts resting in the imagination to gaining the necessary wisdom to successfully complete the demands of every task. Learning how to use imagination properly is a powerful creative quality. Creative thinking brings clarity while visualization carries substance that defines details. Demarcation lines separate those who plan to win and do, and those who never visualize so they continue to lose. Creative thinkers learn to visualize and embrace their imagination by breathing life into the dreams God has entrusted to them. To possess your dream you must imagine it coming to pass. A productive person will skillfully develop a very detailed plan by recording specific steps, that once implemented enable them to accomplish exceptionally great things.

Writing the Plan

Writing the dream down empowers you to physically measure the tangible growth of your dream from its conception as an embryo, watching its development, to giving it birth, then finally, holding the finished product in your hands. A written plan helps you to develop and refine the concepts shown in your dream. Written dreams possess longevity because you are able to focus your attention, time and energy on fulfilling them. Be serious about working hard, and taking possession of your dreams in order to keep them alive. Recording your dream brings an emotional clarity which causes the dream to move from the realm of possibilities' to becoming a probability. Don't be a casual onlooker in life but be thorough, make the needed sacrifices that give import to an idea. A dream is a progressive reality that manifest through the art of visualization.

Visualize the dream or vision until you have conceived it from start to finish in your mind. To make your dream a reality set a specific deadline or target date for achieving each goal. Lay a firm foundation by building off of the life principles found in the Word of God. Design a detailed blueprint, or architectural strategy with a comprehensive list of everything you need to be accomplished by a certain date. Keep progressing by using your colorful imagination to visualize moving forward daily measuring your progress to determine what you can accomplish. If you neglect your dream or stop carrying it with you on a daily basis you can abort the dream, causing it to die prematurely. If you abandon your dream it will die in the womb; never seeing the light of day. To carry a dream full term let it develop over time and continue to push forward until you can safely birth your dream.

Passion

Passion is a natural part of loving life unconditionally. Once you recognize that passion is the substance of life you will thrive. For passion to grow and develop it is important to design a nurturing, dynamic environment where it is safe to express yourself. Passion empowers you to discover the highest path to take in order to pursue your life purpose.

Passion is a powerful tool that makes life worth living. Passion releases the courage to take the necessary risks to ignite your dreams. Anything worth obtaining is going to require a calculated risk in its pursuit. If you desire a friend you must show yourself friendly and hazard the possibility of being rejected or turned down for someone else. If you are single, yet want to get married, you must be willing to risk the pain of a broken heart in order to have the possibility of a happy marriage. But, never settle for less than you truly want.

Compromise becomes the furthermost enemy of greatness when you settle for less than your heart desires. God has placed specific requirements in your heart that He longs to fulfill. If you have to talk yourself into being with someone who possesses fewer virtues or who has poor character most likely you are compromising a godly standard or settling for less than what God has reserved for you. If you will seek God for His perfect will and plan for your life He will reveal it to you very clearly.

Once upon a time, I was dating an athletic, spiritual Christian man, who was very tall, dark and handsome. He was in full time ministry so he had lot of good attributes. But, he also had some very bad ones that I was struggling to overlook. He was divorced, because of having not one, but two affairs and he was in debt. Since God knows everything, I decided to ask the Holy Spirit what His thoughts were on the possibilities of us being a couple.

God often speaks to me through nature so I got my Bible and went to my back porch to read, pray, look and listen. As I loved and adored the Lord; seeking His perfect will and desire for my life concerning marriage and a ministry partner, two ducks flew through the air. They both landed in the alleyway behind my fenced backyard. Suddenly, the beautiful male mallard took flight again and flew over my fence as if to say, "Hello there!" He definitely made a grand entrance to ensure his presence was known. He looked around to see what was available to him in my yard. He was bold and beautiful. With head and chest held high he quacked and strutted his stuff. The unusual thing I noticed was that he was not with another female Mallard. You know the saying, "birds of a feather flock together." He had discarded the gorgeous, pure white duck he had been with in his search for 'greener pastures.' Mr. Mallard quickly discovered my yard contained a bird feeder that attracted various breeds of birds so he had a broad selection of new friends from which to choose. When Mr. Mallard abandoned Mrs. Mallard she became distressed, frantically pacing back and forth, peering through the fence slates. She could only see bits and pieces of what he was doing. She rubbed her beak on the wooden planks desperate to see what was going on inside the fence. She quacked to him but gained no response. I felt so sorry for her. It was as if her heart was broken. She didn't understand why he had 'flown the coop' so to speak. He had placed distance and a fenced boundary between them. She was forlorn, troubled and alone. She was rejected, left without any help as she remained on the outside looking in.

The first thing I asked Holy Spirit was, "Why is a Mallard with a white duck instead of one of his own breed?" "She made him look good for a season as he was able to ride on her spotless reputation." The Holy Spirit reminded me that, "The color white means love, peace, the purity and the holiness of God. White depicts a clean spirit without mixture, white light, righteousness, and a blameless innocence. Barbie the white duck is you." "I have shown you what will take place in the future. Do not be negatively affected, hurt, distressed or disappointed with the way your friend will act. Let his bad decisions roll off of you just like water rolls off a duck's back." The Holy Spirit began to tell me about the characteristics of a male mallard. "The male Mallard duck is a multicolored or mixed dark bird. Mallards are known to frequently interbreed with their closest relatives and other distantly related breeds so they are not very selective in their mating habits, they are 'fowl', thus creating genetic pollution." "When the female lays her eggs and starts nesting, she is left by the male. He deserts her and joins other single males who do not have a mate. These groups of (married and single) males stand by looking for isolated or unattached female ducks to target, regardless of their species. They chase the females until she weakens. Then they peck her neck, hold her down and forcibly take turns copulating with her. This action is called "attempted rape flight" or "rape-intent flights."" I was stunned! The Holy Spirit had issued a strong warning to me that day. "Do not compromise your high standards or even consider marriage with this man, for he is an adulterer." I knew that if I were to marry this person, he would abandon me for another woman, just as he had done to his previous wife. He had not changed his feathers. They were still dark. God always has a plan to prosper us. If we will ask the Holy Spirit He will always direct us from harm's way so that we reach our highest destiny.

Wherever your passion resides, there you will also find your purpose in life. If you continue to walk down the same path in life, you will always obtain the same results. Enthusiastically pursuing what you want out of life is the only path that leads to fulfillment. A person who wants to achieve their dreams should determine where they are currently. Then they need to calculate the time it will take them to be where they want to be in the future. Next they must formulate a plan of action that will carry them to where they want to go. Mental aerobics are misleading because they can produce doubt and fear. When we are excited about life we are able to breakout of common patterns to venture into the extraordinary where others fear to go.

Ten Steps to turn your Dreams into a Reality.

1. Watch, look and listen to what God is showing and saying to you in the vision. Read, contemplate and reflect on the dream.

2. Wait on the Lord in constant prayer and meditation until the Holy Spirit brings clarity to the revelation.

3. Decide what you are called to accomplish in life; then design a personal bucket list of achievements.

4. Imagine and visualize creative ideas that will motivate you to take action. Visually see each step to reach your goals. Want it so bad you can taste it. If it is a reality to you no one can steal it from you.

5. Determine where you want to go, visualize the goals you want as already being achieved.

6. Establish when you want to arrive at your destination goal. Then take the steps that are necessary to figure out how much time it will take to get there.
7. Set a specific list of goals with clear objectives; make a blueprint for your life to avoid the "I wish I had" or "Some day I'm going to" regrets.
8. Do not wait to begin until you understand how it will happen but use your current level of faith. Keep the faith and remain hopeful; doubt, sin and unbelief will destroy the dream.
9. Do not become discouraged or weary if the vision is delayed. Commit to where you want to go and the how to do it will show up.
10. Telling other positive people what your goals and vision are in life will attract people with the same goals and purpose in life to help you along the way.

"Success by the yard can be hard, but by the inch it is a synch." Break down the walls of procrastination by whittling down your big goals into little steps.

What is your plan to be successful? How will you accomplish each segment of your business idea? Developing a mission statement which contains a logical sequence of primary goals is essential to launching a new business or any venture. You will need a written business plan for achieving your goals. Ask yourself, "Am I committed to walking the walk or do I just enjoy hearing myself talk the talk?" Know the broad idea of where you are headed. As you travel this course over time, the specifics of how to narrow the road will manifest and become clearer, leading to success.

Your imagination will carry you to places unknown until your feet are able to walk you there. The imagination should be used to birth and record creative ideas in the mind. There are major components to creative thinking. Once an idea is birthed, it is time to visualize the different aspects until you can see their development. Now, ask God for wisdom to move forward, the Holy Spirit will empower you to resist the urge to procrastinate. Determine to implement and accomplish at least one thing on your daily list. You have to have a plan. People, who fail to plan, subconsciously plan to fail. Creative thoughts and visualization will produce a concrete plan of actions. Greatness is in the inside of you because the Christ who is in you is great!

Visualization

Adapting creative thoughts that are born in our imaginations are like planting a seed that becomes a plant and eventually grows into a stately oak tree that bears fruit. Everything can take shape through visualization; the final achievement is magnificent and gratifying. The four simple steps to success are to imagine grand things, pray and plan with a strategy and then work hard to fulfill your desired goals.

It is important to see your dreams as being obtainable. Each morning when you awaken from a dream, continue to lie in your bed for thirty minutes, to visualize and meditate on the images of the previous night before you get up. It is necessary to use this peaceful time of day to reflect, to arrange your thoughts, to plan and prioritize a productive day. When your feet hit the floor you should know exactly where you are headed so you can move forward with purposeful planning.

Believers should daily practice visualization following their time of prayer and Bible reading. We all need to take time every morning when we are energized, fresh and alert to read the Bible and pray out loud. Visualizing the stories in the Bible will empower the imagination to pull you into the setting to have a personal experience with Biblical characters, angels or an encounter with the Lord. Mornings are the best time to access the creative realm of faith that has been released by the hearing and reading of the Word. Ten times the normal amount of creative energy is released during the night to bring us into a higher productive flow during the day. Once a vision is formulated it is important to capture the vision by creating a vision board or dream wall that displays the pictures and images that best communicate your dream. Collect photographic images as well as keepsakes to help your dreams come to life. Imagine yourself being there as you focus on the pursuit and apprehension of your life goals. Visualization is a powerful means that allows you to see the goal. What you focus your attention on, you empower. So stay focused on the dreams God has given you until they become a reality.

God is the creator of the universe. He is the architect of both the tangible, natural, physical realm; and of the intangible, invisible, spiritual realms. God has given us the power of visualization to see what has not yet occurred in our lives. Visualization is a God-inspired spiritual concept that can change and transform us. Jesus was the master at getting audiences everywhere to visualize the story characters and objects in the life parables He taught. Jesus' disciples grasped new concepts and the understanding of higher spiritual truths through visualizing the parabolic stories that compared the higher spiritual realm to the natural realm. Jesus used the tangible earthly elements such as pearls, coins, fishing nets, corn, sheep, and children, clouds, and wine to help equip people to understand the invisible realms of the kingdom of heaven. Jesus used the principle of contrast and comparisons of objects as an art form. He used everyday objects to empower the mind's eye to expand beyond the familiar things in life to see the intangible possibilities that awaited them. When we are able to see Jesus for who He is, our spirit man has faith to believe that with God nothing is impossible.

Men and women without any formal spiritual training gained knowledge by visualizing the stories God told by using their image center or mind's eye. Depending on the type of crowd Jesus was in front of He would choose the components of the parable He told to meet the specific needs of those people. To farmers and laborers Jesus compared the kingdom of heaven to a mustard seed, or a woman hiding leaven in dough, and a man finding a pearl treasure hidden in a field. When He was in a fishing community He would compare the kingdom of heaven to a drag net cast into the sea to gather every kind of fish. When speaking to property owners Jesus compared the kingdom of heaven to the head of a household who brought out his old and new treasures or a landowner who went out early in the morning to hire laborers for his vineyard. Jesus encouraged His followers to be shrewd as snakes, and wise as a serpent yet He also said we must be innocent as a child to enter the kingdom and as gentle as a dove. He knew that people could not grasp the higher concepts of heaven if they had never been there. But they could understand how a seed germinated and became a fruit bearing tree.

The power of visualization enables us to look beyond the tangible limits of the natural to grasp the certainty of the intangible realm of faith although it has not yet been performed. There is always a silent, unspoken tension between faith and the natural difficulties of producing reality.

God has used visualization throughout history to help people see what the future held for them. God is the author of visualization. It is a principle of God; not a New Age concept or a man made idea. It is a powerful creative principle found throughout the Bible if one has spiritual eyes that see and spiritual ears to hear.

Abram left the familiar and traveled toward an unknown Promised Land but in the process he became impatient and discouraged. Abram's dream was given clarity of a new home and promised child when the audible voice of God directed him to, "Look up into the sky and count the stars." God used visualization through the imagery of stars to strengthen the imaginary hope of a promise yet to be fulfilled. Abram saw his future painted in the innumerable brilliant stars that covered the dark night's sky. Abraham viewed the countless stars and grains of sand to understand the magnitude of the promises that had not yet occurred yet he believed, even though they had not yet been performed. To obtain spiritual promises it is necessary to accept as true that which has not yet been carried out as having already become a reality in another realm. Faith is the conduit that draws the hidden realities of the future into our now. In the kingdom of heaven everything takes place through faith so it is possible to use your imagination to see and enlarge the boarders of your future success.

God helped Abram imagine a grand possibility in order to strengthen the vision contained within his heart. Abram scribed what he visualized when he wrote down the promises God had given to him. His visual experience was recorded in Scripture so he could pass it on to future generations enabling us to glean from the God given spiritual principles of visualization (Genesis 15).

The future belongs to those who believe in the beauty of their dreams. The revelatory images that God gives us in our dreams cause us to stretch up to grasp our visual hopes of tomorrow. Deep inside we have a God given desire to possess our destiny. A vision is a dream that becomes so clear and plain that it is inscribed on the tablets of the heart; when this happens no one can take it away. Visions can propel you from where you are now by launching you into a freshly formed destiny. When we dream big dreams we can see where, when and how we are going to succeed. The power of the imagination is where ideas are born so it is a necessary ingredient to change your life, so dare to dream. Imagination gives us access to every possibility in existence; it is the foretaste of life's coming attractions. All accomplishments and the entirety of earth's wealth had their beginning in the visual dreams of the night.

But, where there is no vision to promote change and bring increase, people perish from boredom. King Solomon who was the world's wealthiest and wisest king said, "If a nation or person is not guided by a God given vision, they will lose self-control, become lawless and perish, but the nation that obeys God's law will prosper and be happy. If people can't see what God is doing, they stumble and fall; but when they attend to what the Holy Spirit reveals, they are most blessed." It is vitally important to give your vision substance to sustain the passion in your heart and mind.

Take a mental picture of where you are right now. Then take another depiction of where you want to go or what you want to achieve in life by a specific time, date or age. Every area in your life affects the other aspects of your life. Finances are an important part of life so it is necessary to save for and invest your time, vigor and money in your future. In order to live a spiritually balanced life of excellence it is important to formulate a comprehensive vision for every aspect of your life. These areas include but are not limited to your work or career choices, investments and savings, health, personal and social relationships, recreation, exercise, and finally retirement in your golden years. If you plan correctly you will be able to retire while you are still young enough to enjoy life. Without a visionary plan mediocrity sets in to steal your potential.

Do you enjoy prosperity and the finer things of life? Or do you feel like you are doomed to remain poor, mediocre and subservient? Jesus prayed that in all respects you may prosper and be in good health, just as your soul prospers by keeping Christ the central focus in your life. If you will create a vision board with pictures of your greatest calling, hopes, and the type of cars, houses, vacation spots, life partner, friends and desires displayed some day they will manifest. A dream wall can serve a very useful purpose. At first it may seem to be a little illusory because the picture images on your wall do not exist in your real world at the moment. But they are real because they exist in the desires of your heart and mind. If you display them, plan and pray about them, with a lot of hard work, they will materialize and become tangible because they are activated by your faith.

What is most important is who you are becoming in the process of achieving life's goals. On your journey you will overcome many road blocks. Quickly quiet the negative thoughts in your head. Continue to remove every obstacle that arises to master the trials of life. The process that leads to success starts with visualization. Find or create a specific colorful picture of your dreams. If your dreams remain a misty vapor they will not inspire results and you will lack incentive.

Visualization is a powerful tool. Researchers have proven that the chemicals and mechanics of your brain cannot discern the differences between the faith realm and the concrete realms of reality. College students who used visualization to accomplish an undertaking ahead of time were 98% successful when it came time to perform that specific task in real time. Those who had not prepared by visualizing their upcoming test only had a 50% success rate. This simple example clearly demonstrates the power the imagination possesses through visualization.

The power of visualization will help you develop your ability to achieve any goal. Take time to picture the landscape of the yard to your dream home. Sit by the pool look over the valley from your mountain retreat or beach resort. See the furniture you dream about replacing what you currently own. If you will visualize your goals as having been successfully completed, the brain will capture those images as a memory. It is easy to plan for what has already manifested or taken place in one's mind. The person who dwells on negative thoughts and images allows fear to destroy their hopes and dreams. Instead focus your faith on the promises God has given you, as well as your hopes of achieving your goals. Use visualization to picture success being obtained so that a brilliant future will materialize to fulfill your life.

It is important to visualize your dreams. Write them down; record them to give your vision longevity. You must make your dreams a reality before you can accomplish them. The reason people never achieve their dreams is because they fail to write them down so they can be seen clearly. The process of completing a vision takes a lot time and effort. For example take the old polarized camera, the snapshot takes just a second; but for the picture to totally develop, it required a good amount of time for the process to reach its maximum clarity with all the colorful details that enhanced the crisp images. When your vision becomes clear, no one can take it away from you. Let your God given vision consume your five senses until it becomes part of you. Allow yourself to hear it, see it, taste it, smell it, and feel it, until you achieve it.

The dreams and visions God births in us bring revelation, illumination, and inspiration. Revelation is the disclosure of divine knowledge and truth that has always been present but not yet realized. The Holy Spirit instantly reveals spiritual knowledge about God and His ways through direct or indirect revelation to a person's spirit.

Revelation is not learned through the intellect (gnosis assumption or scientific, methodical knowledge); it is imparted into the depths of the spirit's (epignosis) intuition, which brings an exact, truthful knowledge. To know God is to experience God. The Spirit of God can not be known by the intellect; for the intellect can only know His attributes. Revelation comes from the Greek word apokalypsis. It means the unveiling of mysteries, which have been hidden or concealed, that are revealed or discovered by removing a covering.

Revelation comes to bring an accelerated transformation. Revelation knowledge births change in the soul; awakening an unmediated spiritual awareness, that forwards one's movements on a higher plane, to grant a quickening of their faith's actions in the Spirit. The spirit realm moves at a much greater speed than the natural realm to allow creative miracles to occur. The mind cannot comprehend the manifestation of the revelation knowledge of the glory of the Lord that is covering the earth (Habakkuk 2:14) but the spirit can.

Knowledge is the Hebrew word yada that is used in (Genesis 4:1). Yada depicted Adam and Eve's lying down together in spiritual intimacy, skillfully showing, revealing their most intimate needs and secret desires without inhibition or reservation, completely trusting that they would find mutual fulfillment while gazing into each other's eyes, and by this observation, learning how to please, respect, comprehend, perceive, and know each other completely; sexually, emotionally, spiritually, and physically. Adam and Eve had to teach one another. They answered their mate's questions, and declared when pleasure was reached. They became familiar with each other's bodies. They discovered and understood what made them feel loved. When the light of their two souls touched through intercourse, they ignited, merged and intermingled to become one. Yada means to learn to know, discover through observation, to discriminate, discern or distinguish between, as one becomes thoroughly acquainted physically, emotionally, and spiritually with the one they love. Revelation knowledge comes when we are intimately acquainted with God's Holy Spirit and His ways, knowing what is pleasing to Him and learning how to bring Him pleasure.

- Gnosis[2], Strong's NT:1108 from NT:1097; knowing (the act), i.e. (by implication) knowledge: KJV - knowledge, science.
- Epignosis[3], Strong's NT:1922), acknowledge a full, or thorough knowledge, discernment, recognition.
- Apokalypsis[4], the Greek meaning "an unveiling" or "a disclosure." (from Bible Knowledge Commentary/Old Testament Copyright © 1983, 2000 Cook Communications Ministries; Bible Knowledge Commentary/New Testament Copyright © 1983, 2000 Cook Communications Ministries. All rights reserved.)
- Yada[5]: Strong's Genesis 4:1, OT: 3045(Biblesoft's New Exhaustive Strong's Numbers and Concordance with Expanded Greek-Hebrew Dictionary. Copyright © 1994, 2003, 2006 Biblesoft, Inc. and International Bible Translators, Inc.)

Revealed knowledge becomes ours experientially when we acknowledge God's presence, surrender to Him by following and obeying His will. Faith and the practice of spiritual knowledge are required to manifest the glory of God. The meat of revelation is for mature people who have experienced and practiced moving in the glory to discern the difference between good and evil (Hebrews 5:14). Without revelation knowledge we will never progress to the next dimension of supernatural glory. The glory realm requires a humble spirit that is motivated by total dependence upon the leading of the Holy Spirit.

Illumination is derived from both spiritual and intellectual enlightenment. Symbolically the bee represents illumination, industry, diligence, and expertise, harmony, wisdom, and sociability. Bees are generous givers and share their lives with others in the community thus they can also represent the power of resurrection. The Old Testament prophetess Deborah's name meant bee or prophetic discourse. Spiritual instruction and guidance bring prosperity to the citizens of eternity when the lamp or the eyes of the body are full of God's light. Spiritual illumination will draw both the light of God's favor and the favor of man upon a person.

Inspiration is the ability to mobilize others by communicating the discovered truths of God so that others can understand and champion the cause for God. To inspire means to inhale, or breathe in the Spirit to stimulate the mind, to create or to activate the emotions to a higher level of understanding. To spiritually inspire is to guide, declare, to reveal the future through the anointed Word of the Lord.

Chapter 7
Faith in the Secret Place

Faith is the gift God gave to everyone. We all have a measure of faith. However, the faith of the believer, allows them to take dominion over the natural realms of space, suspend or accelerate time, and change matter. Faith in God empowers the Believer to cast out devils, heal the sick and diseased. Faith is the spiritual substance that connects us to an eternal God; Who has always been and will always be forever. God is totally independent of time because He does not change therefore God is the same yesterday, today and forever more.

God created the world, universe and realms of light, time, and space for us to learn to navigate because He exists outside of the reality of linear time. Eternal time is cyclical like a spiral staircase that is always ascending to a higher level of glory. An awareness of the Divine gives us the ability to withdraw within our hearts to meet God in the secret place. The prophets, seers, saints and sages of old, the great cloud of witnesses, call to each of us from the pages of the Bible to know God and posses the conscious presence of the faith of God. Yet the church has declined in knowledge of the Holy and surrendered their own lofty impressions of God. Even some of the clergy no longer walk in the fear the Lord but have adopted the ways of the world.

The Scripture reveals a difficult mystery; one day with the Lord is as a thousand years, and a thousand years is as one day and a nation will come to the Lord in a day. For this to be possible, we must access God's glorious presence, heavenly plans, and power.

The glory is the atmosphere of heaven that gives evidence of God's sovereign power manifesting His visible presence to humanity, when, and how, He desires. God's higher thoughts, glorious light, and plans enter our spirit, through our imagination, dreams and visions, to imprint spiritual pictures and blue prints on our subconscious, or image center. God-given dreams are able to anoint us, transforming us into world changers by bringing us revelation knowledge from His heart. The anointing of God empowers us to accomplish the dreams God has given us on earth.

The person who offers thanksgiving and praise in the course of his life, that guards the words of his mouth, and orders his conversations correctly, makes sure he lives a morally up right life, shows God honor by wisely following His ways. When we walk in Gods ways, He will be presently near us at all times, to provide for us and to show us the power of His salvation in our lives and through the visions of the night.

There is a beautiful dwelling place in God, in the realms of His Spirit, the secret place that few journey to find. It is the zero point of the eternal kingdom where the mist of man's spirit touches God's majesty and is then intertwined, mingling with the ever present Spirit of God. Here temporal man meets God's endless splendor. Here man is consumed by God's power and lost in His eternal expanse. Once we are encompassed about by such a great God, we recognize our finite frailty compared to His omnipotence. In this place of divine sanctuary it is obvious we have an inability to comprehend the magnitude of God. But, if we will allow our faith to move to the forefront, engaging with and believing in the love of God, we are drawn into a dimension that is far above our intellect or physical ability to navigate.

Here in the presence of God, the Holy Spirit guides us as we enter into rest, shrouded in the peace of God that passes all understanding. The Holy Spirit teaches us how to move, to breathe Him in and to have the very essence of our very being in Him. In this realm of revelatory vision we are taught to gaze into the Holy Spirit to see the shadow of things God has hidden for us to discover. We quietly listen to hear the sweet melodies of His voice pouring over our expectant heart. Once we behold the concealed vastness of God's supernatural being and perceive the sound of God's plans we are called to act, to obediently mirror the Holy Spirits' behavior to reveal and give voice and movement as the Spirits' desires.

Now faith that is mixed with the Words of God ignites actions that release the mystical realms. The Spirit gently broods over emptiness, flowing into them, filling every space of the vacuous form, until each person is overflowing with abundance and pours forth the substance of God's presence like a powerful river for all to see. When we learn to cooperate with the Spirit of God, He manifests His mighty miracle presence before the world He created.

The creative realm of faith is where things that are not yet substance become tangible as they are spoken into being. Here in this place of tranquility God utilizes us as vehicles to bring the things of the spiritual kingdom out of their holding places, so they can be manifest on the earth. Our prayers, decrees and declarations release the hand of God to establish His presence through us to perform creative miracles, transform lives, supply needs, and grant provision. Words spoken in the realms of faith ignite a spiritual movement or explosion in the corridors of eternity. The proceeding Word of God comes echoing forth at the fullness of time. Angels are dispatched with the power of heaven in their wings. Heaven moves when faith announces its presence in the believing heart of man and it causes us to shift into a higher realm of existence.

When the Holy Spirit comes in righteous judgment, He exposes the error of the godless world's view of sin. Holy Spirit shows humanity that their refusal to believe in Jesus is their basic sin; that righteousness comes only from heaven, where Jesus with the Father, are concealed out of their sight and control; that judgment takes place as the ruler of this godless world is brought to trial and convicted.

Jesus desires to break the silence and reveal Himself to us. He has so much more to give out, describe, show and tell us, but at our current level of spiritual hunger, His conversations are too much for us to accept now at our depth of spiritual understanding. Every time the Spirit of Truth, the Holy Spirit comes, the Friend who honors Jesus, He shows us the way; literally leading us by the hand, teaching and guiding us into all levels of truth.

The Holy Spirit does not draw attention to Himself. He will not speak His own words. He will only declare, rehearse report and show the conversations He hears spoken in the audience of the Father. He has the wisdom and ability to disclose and bring hidden mysteries to light making sense of concealed things, so that we gain understanding of what will take place at another time. The Holy Spirit is always respectful and proper; He breaks the silence to speak to us, giving out truth and describes the revelation of what He hears. He proclaims what will happen in the future.

The Spirit of truth will bring glory to Jesus by telling us what He receives from the throne of God. All that the Father has is given to Jesus. When Jesus calls the Holy Spirit, He comes to violently seize and take hold of the amazing things Jesus shares Him. What the Holy Spirit receives from Jesus, He is free to deliver to us. After a short time in the Holy Spirit's presence we won't be just hopeful spectators, but we will be able to discern, behold, perceive and see Jesus face to face. Then after a little period of time, in another day, we will be mature in the Spirit, so we will intentionally look to see Jesus again with our eyes wide open, voluntarily, earnestly, observing and intensely beholding and inspecting the remarkable things that appear (John 16:8–16).

God loved Jesus from before the foundation of the world. God sent Jesus to this perishing world. Jesus, the Living Word of God, impacted His disciples and also returns to us, in the glory realm, through the Holy Spirit, to speak God's Words of deliverance and healing. Jesus was manifested in the flesh. The Holy Spirit draws people so they may be saved and have the fullness of God's joy in them. Today Jesus still manifest in the flesh but it is through individuals who have sanctified themselves and learned to meet Jesus in the Spirit of Truth.

In the realms of glory, which are similar to the dream realms, Jesus imprints His Words upon the tablets of our hearts, so we become living testimonies of His love, books read by all who met us. Jesus taught His disciples through parables during His earthly ministry. Now that same Jesus teaches every living person through their parabolic dreams of the night. The world hates us because we are holy and consecrated to God; no longer defined by the standards of the world or those who partake in the world's ways; just as Jesus is not of this world. We are seated in heavenly places of glory with Jesus. The Father forms a consecrated truth barrier of glory between us and the evil one. Our mission is to continually stay connected with the glory while we rule, reign and reside in the world.

Believers are one with the disciples, the great cloud of witnesses that has gone before, with Jesus the Word, the Father, and the Holy Spirit even as Jesus is in the Father and the Father is in Him as One. The Father pours His knowledge into Jesus, who transfers it to the Holy Spirit who releases revelation knowledge to us so we can return praise unto the Father. We are in the loop. Thus the mysterious circle of disclosure remains unbroken, connected and continuous.

Unification in love with God and one another will enable the world to believe that we have been sent by God. We share in the one same glory that God the Father gave to Jesus. God's glory matures us into one perfectly unified body; just as the Trinity is One God. When believers walk in one heart and mind, united in love, with God and each other, it gives a godless world evident proof that God is love. God loves the world in the same way He loved and sent Jesus to save the world.

Jesus desires that all believers meet with Him in the realms of glory where He resides so that we can see His glory and splendor. The world does not know God; but Jesus knows who God is and what God does, making all His names and attributes known to us so God's love can dwell within us.

Jesus prayed for our oneness in God. If believers in Jesus continue to lack the reality of a spiritual union with God, not operating in and mirroring the Father's love for Christ to others but remain divided, the world will never come to know the love of Christ and His death will seem to have been in vain. God is love! The last great move of God will come to usher in the final harvest of souls, when the church of Jesus Christ unites as one; learns to first love themselves, then one another and finally their enemies. When we stand united as one, to preach the gospel of the kingdom, in the powerful substance of God's love, His weighty presence will ignite the realms of glory to release signs, wonders and creative miracles. When this supernatural anointing of God's glorious love surrounds our lives and we walk as One New Man, the Kingdom of God will be manifest on earth as it is in heaven. In the presence of God we discover who we were created to be in Christ.

Chapter 8
The Power of Imagination

What is imagination? Can our imagination be used for good and for evil? What is the difference between a self-centered, vain imagination, and a positive, productive, renewed or sanctified, godly imagination? Albert Einstein said, "Imagination is more important than knowledge. Knowledge is limited. Imagination encircles the world."

Imagination is the visionary power of the mind to form mental images or concepts of something that is not really present at that particular time. It is the ability to think, imagine, or create something new that has never been seen or done before. The imagination joined with the power of God's creative Words through prayer, dream interpretation and prophecy has the ability to create things that are not yet visible.

The renewed imagination also has the power to change negative things that are, by creating a new positive alternative. Things, events, objects and ideas that are seen in the imagination can be formed and brought into reality through prayer. Speaking and decreeing the Word of God alerts angels to the spiritual gateways that have been opened to the natural realm. These entry points funnel God's increase and creativity into its rightful place in one's life. Imagination is Godlike in that it is the bold voice of daring enterprise. God dreamed the world and imagined everything that is in it before He released His creative powers through the spoken Word. Imagination rules humanity whether it is an evil, vain, fanciful imagination or imaginations inspired by a loving, all knowing God.

Jacob allowed his unchecked imagination to arouse great fear and run away with his emotions. Like Chicken Little clucking around the barnyard screaming, "The sky is falling," he began to believe the most dreadful outcome. The frightening news of his Brother Esau's approach brought concern for the possible loss of his life, and the demise of his family. Fear causes us to imagine the worst possible scenario while forgetting the promises God has given us. In contrast, faith empowers us to please God by focusing on the potential and not the problems. When we focus on God's perfect love we learn to trust in His provision and all fear is cast away. "And Jacob was greatly afraid and distressed…" (Genesis 32:7). In this passage the Hebrew word for afraid is yare' (yaw-ray') OT:3372; which means to morally fear, to reverence another, or see someone as frightening, to allow the imagination to run wild with dread, to terribly fear a circumstance, action, or situation that has not taken place yet. Distressed is the Hebrew word yatsar (yaw-tsar'); meaning a vexation that causes one to be straightened out, pressed into shape, squeezed through a frame, to be molded by a potter in a narrow place that reforms you into someone else, to make a resolve to change, to be determined to accomplish your purpose, or be fashioned to reach ones' destiny in life. A similar Hebrew word yetser, (yay'-tsar) mean to become distressed because the imagination, has formed a negative concept in the mind.

The choices we make in life determine our destiny. God allows choices of life and good, death and evil, to be set before us. Each choice we make, whether it is big or little, either draws us closer to fulfilling our God given destiny or to aborting the call God has reserved for us. If we are not sure what choice is the right choice, God will give us the wisdom that is needed to choose correctly. Wisdom is the ability to create the perfect conclusion in the perfect way. God's wisdom sees everything in focus from the foundational beginning to the end with flawless precision.

God beckons us to love Him so the fear of the Lord will keep us clean, enduring forever. God is love but it is only one of His many attributes, so it doesn't limit or completely define Him. God is also holy, just, faithful, truthful, kind, immutable. God's love will cover a multitude of sin, until we are able to recognize it as sin and repent. God is infinite, sovereign, and self-existent, eternal and incomprehensible. His love for us disposes Him to desire our best. God's dominion empowers Him to secure the utmost and highest for us. If we keep God's pure commandments, our eyes will be enlightened. His statutes and true judgments enable us to walk in righteous, godly ways, even in our imagination.

The principles of the Lord are right, producing a heart full of joy. The laws of God are perfect; so they have the power to restore the psyche. In keeping God's way, there is great reward. When we are obedient, we live in abundance and multiply in every direction. The blessings of God cause us to possess the promises. The authentication of the Lord is sure. By conducting one's life by His example, the simple are made wise. Jesus is the Living Word. He is our example. The Word was made flesh and came to walk and talk with man. Now the Living Word continues to dwell in the hearts of those who love Him. We can find God in the secret place and lean on our Beloved.

The Word of God is not mysterious or far off. It is not concealed in heaven so one has to ascend into the heights to bring it down, to hear or do it. Neither is the Word buried as a treasure, hidden in the depths of the sea. The Word of God is so near. It is in the mouths of earthen vessels, hidden in our hearts that we can perform it and prosper. The power of a prosperous life or the barrenness of death is within the words we speak. Our life is formed from the scenarios we paint in our imagination. When a seed of thought is conceived, it is impregnated with life. The more we water that thought, the more that thought grows. When that thought reaches maturity, it is birthed and becomes a reality. This is why it is paramount that our thoughts remain focused upon the pure, beautiful and positive.

My prayer is, "Lord let the words of my mouth be few and the mediations of my heart be pure and acceptable in Your sight. Help me to discern my errors and exonerate me of hidden faults. Keep me from being presumptuous and do not let sin rule over me. Remove indiscretion far from me, so I am unblemished in Your sight. Rid me of impurities until I am holy and without contaminates. Remove my sin so their ink does not stain the fabric of my being. Then pour me out as a jar of pure refreshing water. Be my rock, my defender and my knight in shining armor." Amen.

Those who live by the rule of the Spirit of life, in Christ, are set free from the act of sin, which leads to death. If we think on earthly or sensual desires, we will walk according to the flesh and reap death. The flesh is carnal and unreceptive towards God's spiritual ways. The flesh cannot please God. Do not walk through life according to the desires of the flesh, but according to the Spirit.

Some boldly commit sin openly or with a blatant heart of intent while others think they are committing sin in secret, assuming their sin is hidden in darkness, away from the gaze or knowledge of others. However, there are always the spiritual eyes and ears of the angels, the great cloud of witnesses and our beloved family members who have gone on before us, that witness and record both our positive and negative behavior. When we are struggling with temptation, heaven dispatches reinforcements to strengthen our spiritual resolve to resist. They come to add their spiritual support to our failing determination. They rejoice when they witness us overcoming temptation. But, if we fail to overcome and indulge in our hidden sin, these same spiritual witnesses will be called to testify against us on judgment day if we do not repent.

When a person is given a chance to repent and they refuse, their spirit is dulled; the heart is hardened and their nature is distorted. The memory of their sin, guilt and shame is always present before them. To escape the reminder of their sinful state they turn to sex, drugs or alcohol to ease their pain. The sinner runs from the torment of God's loving light while plunging into more darkness, until they feel hopeless, buried in the depths of addiction. If a person dies in their sin, those sins are eternally imprinted upon their spirit as darkness, spots or blemishes.

Jesus shed His blood on Calvary so our sins could be forever removed. But if we refuse to ask for forgiveness and repent of our sin, the blood Jesus shed does not profit us. When we turn our faces away from God and ignore such a great salvation, we choose death. God has never sent anyone to hell. In His great love, God sent His only Son, Jesus, to die on a cruel cross so we could choose forgiveness from sin and obtain eternal life. Eternal life is knowing and loving the only true God. People of their own free will choose sin, death and hell.

What would happen if God granted permission for the vilest of sinners to enter heaven without being born again? Could that person tolerate God's living light in his dead, perverted, dark state? Could his dull, sin-hardened conscience turn towards God and repent? Would he be able to enter in to remain in heaven with God's radiance illuminating every flaw, sin and impurity? Could he tolerate being known to such a degree of completeness that it would cause agony and self-loathing?

Such a person would seek to remove himself from God's presence. Without being born again and having his sins removed, heaven would become hell (John 3:3). His life of sin would cause him to retreat back into darkness to escape a loving God. His own sinful heart would choose to spend all eternity doomed to darkness. The sinner chooses the depravity of sin and resides in darkness. Yet, because God, the Father of Light, created him to dwell in eternal light, he will not find happiness in hell's darkness or in heaven's eternal light. The righteous choose to dwell at the level of enlightenment they have received through revelation knowledge; so wherever they find themselves there is joy and contentment (Philippians 4:11).

God in His great grace will reveal Himself to each individual according to the level of their desired aspiration and spiritual aptitude. The Old Testament priest Eli is a good example of God having to adjust His level of appearing due to Eli's spiritual dullness and blindness. Eli was fat and lazy. Eli lacked hunger for God and he neglected to discipline his household. So Eli lived during a time when the revelation of God was rarely heard or seen. Eli's physical eyesight had grown weak and his spiritual eyesight had grown dim mirroring his religious loss of vision.

Thus the light of the Lord's lamp also waned to the point of vanishing to match Eli's narrow sight. His nonchalant dishonoring attitude toward a holy God ended in judgment. God raised up a new order of seers through Samuel who could both hear the clarion voice of the Lord and see the manifested presence of God's bright light (1 Samuel 3:1–3).

The Spirit of God dwells where the mind is set on the Spirit. The Spirit produces liberty, life and peace. When the mind is liberated, it is able to create and function in the miraculous, above the laws of nature. God is able to inspire a renewed mind with His higher thoughts. When we understand God's higher thoughts that come to us in our prayers, dreams and visions, we are able to walk in an advanced or elevated spiritual way of life. Enoch is an example of someone who communed intimately with God.

Faith in God took Enoch into another realm of reality. Enoch agreed and walked with God. His mind was so transformed by the presence of God, that Enoch was no longer recognizable, he was not found. He became a new being by the renewing of his mind. Enoch was no more. God took Enoch up into the heights of heaven because he was found pleasing in God's sight. Enoch was able to avoid our last enemy, death. Enoch learned the ways of eternal life by walking in God's shadow.

When we come to God, we must first believe that He is God! To seek and find God, we must do so with all our heart. Without a heart full of faith it is not possible to please God. Once we find God we must continue to pursue and desire to know the vast depths within Him. We pray, search and yearn for God seeking Him day and night. When Moses sought to know God's grace and favor he asked God to show him His ways of glory (Hebrews 11:5–7). Yet when one takes a step towards God, in God's great mercy, He strides forward to save the spiritually blind and delivers the morally lost. When God finds us bound in the darkness of sin, He saves us so the process of renewing the imaginations of the mind can begin.

Jesus took imagination to a whole new level when He said; "Everyone who looks at a woman with the intent to lust after her has already committed adultery with her in his heart; for as a man thinks in his heart, so is he." It is important to guard the concerns of the heart, for out of the heart flows the matters of life. Those who maintain an uncontaminated heart and unsoiled hands will see God. Those with a vain or evil imagination will bring lack and destruction on themselves. Imagination can carry us to worlds that never have been, but without imagination, we remain complacent and go nowhere.

The natural limits of life are removed when one enters into the realm of imagination. Imagination allows us to experience things that are not limited to the perception of our five natural senses. Through our imagination we can gaze upon what other's eyes cannot see. We can listen to the melodies and lyrics other's ears cannot hear. Imagination is a powerful visionary tool that causes healing and wholeness to enter one's life.

The heart of compassion can be touched with the feelings of other's infirmities. We can bring healing into the lives of those around us when we allow God's love to flow through us. The gift of healing is empowered by compassion for those in pain. Imagination enables a person to visualize themselves completely whole and pain free. Instead of focusing on the negative words of the doctor's report and rehearsing all the disease symptoms, reading and researching all the harmful prognosis of death and deterioration, focus on the creative, life-giving Words of God. The authoritative Word of God has the miraculous power to heal.

Begin to see yourself as strong, whole, pain free and happy, living a full, prosperous life again. Maintain a thankful heart of gratitude towards God for who He is then reflect on the many things He has already done on your behalf. In God's loving kindness He sent Jesus the Living Word to heal and deliver us from destruction. The Word of God has the power to destroy sickness, disease and poverty creating health, wealth and prosperity in its place.

A Healing Angel Visits December 2009

In December, 2009 my lower back went out of alignment. This began shooting, debilitating, and piercing pain throughout my body for no discernable reason. Any type of movement, breathing, walking, standing, lying down and sitting were all very painful. After a day of unending pain I carefully climbed into bed for the night. Resting in my bed, I snuggled in with my little four pound Pomeranian, Super Duper Mini Cooper to reflect on the activities of the day.

Earlier that day during an office visit, my friend, Dr. Waters had shared about his angelic encounter. He had been suffering with great pain. When he was not able to bear the pain any longer, he drove himself to the emergency room for treatment. When he finally arrived back home he was so exhausted that he fell into a deep sleep and had a vision. In this vision he saw an angel that mirrored himself. It had his short crew cut hair and facial features. We both felt like the angel he saw must have been his guardian angel who was sent to bring his healing.

Before I fell asleep, I whispered a simple prayer to the Lord, please send my angel to remove this pain and heal my back tonight. Sleep avoided me due to my severe lower back pain. Despite my discomfort, sometime during the night I finally dozed off. I was awakened at 1:31 a.m. (Luke 13:11–13) The Scripture that goes with that waking time is, *"And behold, there was a woman who had a spirit of infirmity eighteen years, and was bent over and could in no way raise herself up. But when Jesus saw her, He called her to Him and said to her, "Woman, you are loosed from your infirmity." And He laid His hands on her, and immediately she was made straight, and glorified God."* I heard my bedroom door gently opening. At first, I thought my brother Steven, who used to share a home with me, may have come to check on me during the night to see if I needed anything. But, it was not Steven it was a handsome angel. That is when my precious dog, Mini Cooper, sprang into action. He mustered all the strength his little furry body could gather and began barking out an alarm. I tried to quietly comfort Cooper as the angel continued to advance. "Its o.k. Cooper, it is God's angel coming to heal me. Cooper we don't bark at the angels. They are always welcome in our home." God had answered my prayer and sent an angel to take my pain away.

A supernatural peace entered my bedroom. As the beautiful presence and atmosphere of heaven's light permeated the air the pain in my back began to ease. The angel walked across my bedroom floor. He sat on my little prayer couch next to my bed. I felt such comfort and love from this celestial being. His large blue eyes were so compassionate and kind. The strong sculptured features of his face were framed by thick, short blonde curls. He did not speak any words or touch me. I just knew in my spirit he had come to bring God's healing presence in answer to my prayers. There are differing tongues or spoken languages. There are tongues of angels, men, nations, kings, multitudes, and peoples. Although angels are versed in their own language, and the various languages of people, a lot of times they simply communicate through thoughts in the realms of the Spirit. This may include audible languages or not.

Angels don't need to open doors to enter rooms. They are spirits and can walk through walls, doors and any natural substance or structure. I felt that the angelic visitation was as much for Mini Cooper's training as it was for my healing. He was being trained to respond correctly to heavenly guest in my home. The next morning when I awake I noticed that my bedroom door was closed again. The angel let himself in and out through the door. Often angels will just appear in different places. I felt that it was significant that my angel opened the door to enter and then shut the door when he left. God is opening doors for His beloved that no man can shut, Isaiah 45:1. When we use our imaginations in a correct way healing comes on the wings of angels.

Imagination is the creative realm where anything becomes possible. Imagination removes every boundary that restrains or limits productivity. Imagination brings a whole new world into existence that can be seen and experienced through the mind's eye. One can examine different scenarios in their imagination concerning the outcome of past, present or future events.

The world of words allows one to form mental images of things that have not been perceived by the senses as real. The mind constructs mental scenes that are full of substance and proceedings from the past, the present or future. Imagination is the ability to deal with or confront reality with the creative, resourceful power of the mind. A strong imagination empowers one's ability to reconstruct the framework or enlarge the doors of access to prosperity. The imagination makes it possible to experience the possibilities of a new world within the building blocks of the thoughts of the mind.

Everyone is able to develop their imagination. Imagination is not limited to the five physical senses of taste, visual enlightenment, physical sensations, smell, auditory enhancement or an emotional stance. As one's imagination is expanded and taught, they can view situations from various vantage points to obtain creative mental clarity. Positive mental clarity enables a person to see their heart's desires being fulfilled by overriding unpleasant images or circumstances. The heart's desires are first visualized in the mind's eye. Then our request can manifest in the natural realm through faith in God. With much prayer and a healthy, positive mindset that expects great things, success will be obtained.

A godly imagination has the power to release the impossible to manifest in time. I believe in the creative power of a godly imagination. What we can see with our spiritual eyes is immeasurably more important and real than what we can see with our natural eyes. The visionary sight of imagination brings the substance of things that are hoped for into existence. Dreaming is seeing! Seeing is faith believing! I have always believed I can become whatever I can imagine. If you can see it in your imagination, with God's help, and a strong work ethic, you can achieve it in life. Everyone who has achieved great things in life has been a grand dreamer. They purposefully imagine what their ideal future can be and then they systematically work towards obtaining their distant goals or vision. "You are never too old to set another goal or to dream a new dream." Les Brown

Can you imagine what your life would be like if you were able to achieve all God has destined you to become? It is possible to be all God has planned for you. To discover God's plan for your life; allow extended times for meditating on God and daydreaming about His Word. Prayerful times of reflection will enable God to enlighten your mind and work through your imagination. The Holy Spirit will show you all the possibilities that have been positioned ahead of you. Logical people lean on rationale and philosophy, but they starve their imagination and become bored with life. God can take the little, breathe upon it, and make it much, by releasing the multiplication factor to those who possess a thankful, expectant heart.

Memory is the expression of imagination. It is ability to retain or recall things or events that have been imagined or experienced in the past. Memory lost is the obsession or passionate dream one fails or refuses to remember.

Foresight is the act of looking forward with a careful, thoughtful regard for the future. It is the ability to imagine things that can take place in the future. The presence of the Holy Spirit teaches our spiritual eyes of faith to see into the invisible. God grants us visionary access to walk into a reality that is superior to the natural realm where we exist most of the time. Once we gain God's vision for our future we are able to prophesy it into existence. If we will take a leap into the future, boldly decree the things we see from God's perspective, He will establish them for us. The Holy Spirit reveals knowledge that supersedes the rational of carnal reasoning and possesses an internal power that transforms us from the inside out.

Focused faith will cause one to realize the profound possibilities that exist in the invisible realm. Faith gives us access to the invisible realms of the spirit so we can erase the borders of limitation. The fundamental fact of existence is that faith and trust in God is the firm foundation that makes life worth living. The world was called into existence through faith in an unseen God. He commanded creative words to reveal the concealed and bring it forth into being.

Faith that is mixed with hope brings forth the fertile ground of a new reality out of the invisible realm of nothingness. Faith reveals the plans God has concealed in His heart. The heart that diligently seeks for God will instruct us in the night season. The imagination finds pleasure when it sees something that is new or exceptional. When we maintain our focus on the Lord, we are able to rest in hope, knowing we have a good inheritance. When we bless the Lord, the Holy Spirit gives us counsel and shows us the path of abundant life. Entering God's presence releases the fullness of joy so we can experience the pleasures of God forevermore.

The curious soul yearns to explore innovations and pioneer the unknown. The unknown is an open-door that invites us to participate in engineering a new life. In sculpting our brilliant futures we will encounter the unexpected as we dwell in, and walk through dimensions that are beyond our control. This season of discovery brings us to the realization that our steps are ordered by the only, all-knowing, powerful, loving God. He pours out grace, mercy and revelation knowledge to empower us to embrace the new journey every morning. Creative ideas flood the imagination, bringing gratification and delightful surprise to the ardent searchers, as they behold amazing sights that have never before been possessed, documented or even known in existence.

Faith is the spiritual substance that brings proof to the unseen eternal realm of promise and possibilities. Faith makes real the things we hope for. Faith is the proof of what we cannot see. The things we see were made by God, who cannot be seen with our natural eyes. Faith must see through the eyes of understanding with a spiritually enlightened heart. Faith in God's Word enables our mind to be renewed by the Spirit to think like God. When our mind and heart are renewed by hearing the Words of the Holy Spirit, we become active doers of the Word.

Revelation is the meat of the Word, illuminated by the Holy Spirit, Who comes to us as rhema or a now expression of God. Faith connects us to the Spirit of God and moves us into the moment. While focused faith maintains our position as we wait for the promise to manifest. God's Word lays a broad, strong foundation in our life for Him to build upon. God dwells in fragile earthen vessels (2Corinthians 4:7). God desires to set up His habitation within us. When God possesses us, we will imitate Him. We reflect or emulate that which we believe. Faith will cause the invisible power of imagination that is focused on the kingdom of God to manifest in and through our life.

God the Father grants us the spirit of wisdom so we can discern the future. We are instructed to have faith in God. We must also have the faith of God to see mountains of opposition removed from our life. God does not doubt. He knows and believes that the things He says are already finished and accomplished; they will be done; they will come to pass. Therefore we must adopt this powerful, godly life principle. Whatever we ask, when we pray, believe that we receive it and we will have it. To receive answers to our prayers, we need to pray in the names and character of God. Pray and believe that you have God's answers. See things through God's perspectives of grace. When we agree with the grace in God's heart, He will give us the desires of our heart. When sin abounds the world is terrorized, but when God's grace thrives the world is given a renewed hope in a prosperous future.

If we do not agree with God's supernatural ways and plans, our imagination moves out of the higher realms of the spirit, into the inferior natural realms of doubt and unbelief. When doubt reigns, faith is then limited to the temporal, that which we see with our natural eyes or know in our intellect. Unbelief sets a narrow limit on our achievement by defining what we believe is possible, so nothing great can be accomplished.

Holy Spirit gives us the spirit of revelation so we can obtain godly knowledge. Knowledge empowers us to move from the unknown or unseen realm of the invisible into God's revealed will. Revelation creates spiritual motion revealing God's current plans and desires. By revelation, the Holy Spirit makes the mysteries of Christ known to us. When we correctly discern the movement of the Holy

Spirit with the eyes of our heart, we are enlightened. Once we are enlightened, we are transformed from faith to glory, enabling us to expand the kingdom of God. Our complete trust is placed in Christ, who knows the hope He has placed upon our life's calling as believers. The true riches in glory, which are only obtainable through the realms of the Holy Spirit releases power for the imagination to see that which is invisible, interpret dreams and operate in signs, wonders and miracles. Without revelation knowledge, we will never experience the power of God flowing through us.

One of God's greatest gifts to mankind is the power He has instilled within each one of us to create a beautiful life through the power of the imagination. God has given us the ability to imagine the way we would like things to be in our lives and in the world at large. When we take time to enter into a peaceful state of rest, focused on God's love and desire, we can see images of the wonderful spiritual environment God has created for us to exist in. We are able to picture God's provision and plans to prosper us coming to us on the waves of our imagination.

To visualize God's plans is one of the first steps in having those provisions actualized in our lives. Sight, both physical and spiritual, is the gift that forms an access gate for our faith to enter in, connect to the realm of Spirit and then apprehend that which we need. When we lift up our heads to see God's plans through the vision realm and His provisions through the realm of dreams, prayer or with our imagination, we begin to tap into the immensity of the power of God's thoughts towards us.

We are the ancient gates that were created to allow the King of Glory to manifest Himself in the earthly realms. God's heavenly thoughts and ways to success are higher than our earthly traditions, habits and conduct; they are beyond our natural thoughts and limited ways. For us to enter into a greater realm of understanding, to apprehend more, we must exercise our godly imaginations to begin to even scratch the surface of the greatness God has planted within each of our spirits through the indwelling presence of Christ.

In the realm of imagination we see the creative power that God's Word demonstrates when it is joined with faith that sees. We watch (visually imagine) as the rain and snow (God's Word) water the earth, igniting the seeds (prayer) we have sown in the field (world). That which we have planted in faith germinates, buds and produces to bring in a multiplied harvest, much more than we (asked, thought, or imagined) planted. The heavenly water supplies seed for the sower and bread for the eater that remains with us on the earth. As with the water of heaven so is the Word of heaven. When our imaginations see the Word's of God's mouth go forth in action they will create and manifest the greater works upon the earth.

What is more important, man's religion or a personal relationship with God? Our religious traditions and inadequate understanding of the power of God's Word to create has formed such a narrow, restricted corridor for the Holy Spirit to dwell. The whole earth is groaning, crying out for the manifestation of the Son's of God to appear. Those who learn to unleash the creative realms of God through seeing His mighty acts through the power of their imagination will appear as the Son's of God. When we begin to relate to God in His grandeur, letting Him out of the small religious box we have limited Him to, we will see the level of Spiritual manifestations we have never seen before. Can you imagine how great our God is? No matter how great, grand or glorious we imagine God to be, He is exceedingly abundantly beyond our greatest ability to imagine.

God's Audible Voice

My father, Douglas H. Breathitt was a successful, respected Christian attorney; so I was raised in an ultra conservative Presbyterian church with all the proper social etiquettes. They did not believe in or embrace a current day move of the Holy Spirit; as a matter of fact I never remember Holy Spirit's name being mentioned. The spiritual gifts, miracles, signs or wonders were never mentioned from the pulpit only God or Jesus. No matter how rigid and religious they were, I experienced salvation (the greatest miracle of all) in that church, listening to flannel board stories about Jesus and His disciples in Sunday school. I fell in love with Jesus the minute I was introduced to Him. I desired a personal daily encounter with Jesus where I could walk and talk with Him just like the Apostles of old had done. I would imagine what it would have been like if I had been born when Jesus walked the earth doing miracles. I wanted to be one of Jesus' disciples and do the same miracles they did.

Most of the people who attended my church were elderly, sick and weak so I knew they would benefit from the miracle Jesus I heard about in Vacation Bible School. As Mrs. Miley and Mrs. Childs recounted the miracle stories of Jesus to us, describing the events line by line, I was able to enter into the ancient scenes to observe and relive the accounts of the Bible. I believed that some day those incredible events would happen at my church too! But, unfortunately, the services were always the same, scripted and planned. Everyone received a bulletin that informed them of the service outline when they came so everything was very ordered. The only action we saw was when one of the deacons would say "Amen!" out loud from the back of the church. If he said amen more than twice during a service the elders would move in and touch him on the shoulder to ensure things remained decent and in order.

The service had an opening prayer, two hymns, one fast, one slow, with certain stanzas sung, a brief sermon with three points and a current day story illustration, with a closing prayer or benediction. Finally, the pastor would walk from the pulpit, stand at the front door to shake each of our hands as we left the sanctuary showering him with accolades and compliments. Church had very little Jesus content. It was mostly a social event with a religious list of do's and do not's. Church was so predictable, I became bored and uninterested yet I struggled to remain hopeful that some day Jesus would show up. My continuous question was, "Where was the Jesus I fell in love with? And, "Why didn't He ever do the stuff?"

One Sunday morning, I halted the hand shaking procession long enough to ask the Pastor that very question, "Pastor, 'When are we going to do the stuff Jesus did in the Bible?'" "What stuff are you talking about?" he asked. "You know like opening blind eyes, healing deaf ears, the lame walking, and the dead being raised back to life?" God knows our church needed some resurrection power every Sunday because it was full of the frozen chosen or what seemed to be the walking dead. If someone had called an ambulance to come remove the person who had suffered a heart attack from the service, they would have had a difficult time determining which of the congregation were unconscious, dying, dead or just sleeping. My hopes of adding some excitement or relevance to the service was dashed by the pastor's negative response. While patting me on the head in a condescending way, he replied, "Young lady that dispensation is over!" Like a child would know what the word dispensation meant. I just hoped a dispensation wasn't contagious because it sounded terrible and I didn't want it touching me. He continued, "Jesus only did miracles during the times of the apostles. When the last apostle died that time in history came to an end. Jesus could heal if He wanted to but, He just chooses not to heal any more." "We have the Bible now, so we don't need miracles." I remember all of my hopes of being able to know a real live Jesus died in that devastating moment. My faith dropped and anger began to rise in its place. Questions like, "Why did Jesus change?" "Why did He love people more back then than He loves us now?" "Does He still love us?" flooded my mind, and more concerns like, "Does Jesus care about me?" If that's true then, "Why couldn't I have been born in the times of the disciples?" "If Jesus has changed and does not relate to us personally anymore, why should I go to church or serve Him?"

From that tragic Sunday on things changed for the worse in me! There was no longer any hope of Jesus actually showing up one Sunday to save, heal or deliver somebody. I didn't enjoy church any more. So, instead of fighting to stay awake during the long, boring sermons I settled in on the back row, got comfortable, rested my head on the wall and went to sleep. If I wasn't sleeping, I made good use of my time by catching up on my homework. Other times, I would lead the elder's children to skip the service with me. We would walk to Pizza Hut to share a pizza.

One sunny day, while out riding my horse "King," I asked God, "Why He had changed when people still needed Him so desperately in their lives?" I was busy rehearsing all my questions when suddenly I heard someone call my name "Barbie!" I was startled to say the least because there were no people around me. King and I were out running in an orange grove. I remember looking at my horses mouth thinking wouldn't it be wonderful if 'King' had called my name like 'Mr. Ed' the talking horse on T.V.! While I was still watching King's mouth I heard my name called again but the horse's mouth remained still. Again, a third time just like the child Samuel, my name was called a third time. But this time, the audible voice continued to speak by answering the questions I was rehearsing in my heart. "Barbie, I change not! I am the same yesterday, today and forever! If, you will only believe, the same anointing that flowed through the Apostles' of old will flow through you in signs, wonders and miracles."

Suddenly, it did not matter what the church or the pastor had said about Jesus, or what he believed Jesus could and would not do. Because now, I had it straight from the horse's mouth so to speak. When the audible voice of God quotes Scripture (Hebrews 13:8), and gives you an invitation to be just like one of His Apostles, who could possibly doubt or question His integrity any more? From that day forward I was transformed into a believer. I read the Bible with an understanding that anything the Apostles of old were able to do I could do too! The only difference was I was called to do the "greater works" because we live in the best of times. I knew beyond a shadow of a doubt that God was real. Jesus still heals, delivers and does miracles today. Jesus was just looking for someone who would believe in Him, knowing that His Word is still true today, no matter what man may say.

It is time for us to take the limitations off of the God we serve to give expression to the immensity of His power. Let's develop our imaginations so we can dream God's sized dreams. Let's give a free rein to God's colossal presence in a world that is desperate for His manifestations. Who is this King of Glory? He is the Lord of the host of heaven, strong and mighty! It is time we get to know God according to the way He has designed us to know Him, through the largeness of our imaginations, in Spirit and in truth, with our minds renewed according to the Spirit of the power of His Word.

When we worship God in Spirit and in truth, we are able to see with the eyes of our spiritual imagination. Faith allows us to access what is available in the realms of the invisible. Once we imagine a thing, it can be drawn into actuality. Holy Spirit opens the realms of vision so we can see His heart's desire and speak them into existence. We become the channel the Holy Spirit flows through to bring heaven to earth. When we give expression to the move of the Holy Spirit, His power and presence will manifest on earth.

God is the Creator who formed and fashioned the universe through the spoken Word. God brought His dream of creation into existence. He imagined a magnificent universe and a world full of beautiful landscapes, raging oceans, brilliant sounds and majestic creatures. God breathed His life giving Spirit into Adam. God's spiritual DNA gave Adam the ability to speak things into existence. Adam had the power to imagine the characteristics and functions of each animal. Whatever Adam named the animal it became. God creates unique individuals in His image, none of us are ordinary. We are created in God's image with the ability to generate and fashion things in our mind through the imagination. Anything that has ever been created was first thought of or imagined in someone's mind. What have you been called to imagine and prayerfully bring into existence?

In Christ we can be renewed in the spirit of our mind, becoming a new person who operates in righteousness, truth and holiness in the likeness of God's attributes. Imagination reveals truth that our current reality has obscured. Our true spiritual life begins when we awake and live out our dreams. Sadly, some true stories are never realized because it takes courage and an ability to calculate and take risks to live a bold life.

The strength of the Father's great glory gives us the power to be strong in our spirit. When our spirit man is strong, the love of Christ lives in our heart through faith. We begin to imagine and understand the greatness of the depths and heights of His love. When we are possessed by God's love we can be filled with the divine nature and everything God has promised us. When God's transforming love is working within us, God can do exceedingly, abundantly, above all we can ask, think or imagine.

Tragically, most people do not know how to freely accept, understand or receive God's love thinking they must earn God's love through works. They do not know how to interpret the illustrated love letters God sends in their dreams. Individuals who know how to use their imagination in a godly, productive way are in the minority.

People have been taught that the imagination is evil or ungodly, but, everyone uses their imagination in some way every day. Sometimes we worry, imagining the worst possible scenario taking place in our lives and our dreams reflect this attitude. One is never as fortunate or as ill-fated as one imagines. We must learn to live out of a godly imagination, not from our painful history. Most people fearfully focus on the problems that haunt their life rather than magnifying God, who is the creator and giver of life. When we magnify God, He becomes bigger than the problems we face. When we prayerfully focus on God, He is drawn into the situation. When the light of God's presence comes, we are delivered from the darkness of difficulty, sin and sickness. Jesus rebuked Peter because he was not setting his mind on God's interests, but on man's.

Prayer is communing with and seeking God with our whole heart. Prayer is speaking forth God's plans and focusing on His purposes for our life. God's plan is to totally restore us, prosper and give us a hope and a bright future.

Prophecy, which is the testimony of Jesus, is able to open spiritual gateways to give vision for the future. When the hearing of God's Word is infrequent, vision is rare. When we hear and obey God's Word allowing it to conform us to His image, we become visionaries and achievers of His Word. When we walk in His likeness we are able to cast vision. When people do not hear God's voice, they lose hope. Without a vision people perish. Hearing God's voice and seeing His plans releases hope for the future. Vision is God's blue print to prosperity. When we magnify God and call upon His name, He supplies the needed answers and delivers us from hopelessness and all fear. God, and God alone, holds the solutions to the difficulties of life. Imagination can help us visualize and discern the greatness of God so we can walk in His shadow all the days of our life.

Whatever we focus on we will empower, be it positive or negative. Whatever we study or center upon we will draw into our realm of influence or experience. Job said it this way, "That which I feared or saw happening ahead of time has come upon me." The imagination has the ability to draw constructive elements or destructive forces into our life. What we think on will become evident and visible. Whatever we behold we become.

To truly prosper we must fill our minds with God, think on and meditate on the goodness of God. Focus on positive things that are true, right, pure, noble, honorable, reputable, authentic, and compelling— the best, not the worst; the beautiful, gracious and lovely, not the ugly things that distract or curse. Imagination gives us wings to soar above.

Constantly dwell on those things that are of a good character, excellent and praiseworthy so the God of peace will be with you. We should maintain a gentle spirit towards man and a joyful heart of thanksgiving towards God. Prayer requests and thanksgiving cause God to draw near.

Thankful persistence in impossible circumstances will manifest miracles. Jesus gave God advanced thanks for raising his friend Lazarus back to life after he had been dead for four days. Jesus told His friends "Did I not say that if you believed Me you would see God's glory manifested?" Then turning His heart towards heaven, Jesus prayed, "Father, I thank You that You always hear Me. So I offer my thanksgiving to You so that these standing here will hear and believe that You have sent Me and learn to offer You thanksgiving in every state of affair." The power of offering thanks to God in every situation is so powerful that it can raise the decaying dead back to life.

Don't be upset or worried. Negative emotions will only drain your strength and God given creative power to solve problems. Instead of fixating on the problem and racking your nerves, simply pray about everything. Let God know your concerns, recall and thank God for being God and for the things He has already done. Allow the peace of God to invade your thought processes. Sense God's wholeness, knowing everything will come together for good. Christ will displace worry and fear when you invite Him to become the center of your life.

God is real. When we are in God's presence, fear is replaced by a peace that surpasses the natural understanding. To understand is to forgive failures, even one's own. The imagination gives us the power to transcend natural circumstances. God's peace will guard our hearts and minds as we live in Christ. We must practice the spiritual truths we have received, learned, heard and seen in God. He alone is able to make everything work together for our benefit.

God's existence will cause His most excellent harmonies to fill our life and imagination. The thankful heart does not create but helps us find God's omnipresence once we are awaken and regenerated from our mortal slumber.

Imagination is not the same thing as faith. Imagination develops unreal images that are created in the mind and then attempts to bring their existence into reality. Faith does not create; it simply releases what is already there in the invisible realms to manifest. There is a reckoning that must take place in the heart of the believer that recognizes the things they have suffered in life are nothing to compare to the great glory that will be revealed and given to them. The concrete natural and vaporous spiritual worlds are both real. They wait for us to realize that we are the sons of God, called to manifest His powerful presence, transformed as His children doing the greater works.

The invisible spiritual realm of faith is always here, presently bidding us to trust its vaporous appearing; placing it on a superior platform to the natural world we live in, to continually observe and experience life through our senses.

Repentance removes the scales from our eyes so the invisible realm can begin to come into a focused reality. The natural is the enemy of the divine supernatural, the invisible wars with the visible, the real battles with the imagined and the temporal fades in the presence of the eternal. The believer lives a life that places their faith in the unseen. He that comes to God must believe that He is. God is a rewarder of those who diligently seek Him.

The power of the Scripture releases truths that continually manifest when they are mixed with faith beholding God's light. Reality is God! Believing in God, who is three persons in One, also enables us to believe in Jesus and the Holy Spirit. To follow God in His kingdom we must develop the sensitivity of our spirit to follow His gentle promptings. God's kingdom is now; it is presently within us, not reserved for some far off future time. We are come unto the city of a living powerful God, surrounded by an innumerable company of angels and the spirits of just men in the great cloud of witnesses.

The soul sees with spirit eyes and the soul hears with spirit ears. The soul touches with the feelings of compassion and heals with the power of God's might. The more we attune our spiritual senses on being obedient to God's Word the more precise they become. The Word of God will purify our heart to taste and see the goodness of God in the land of the living.

God's true light energy and power is released within us to shine a constant beacon that guides others to His eternal presence. God is here. The presence of God dwells in the heart of His creation. David wrote "Where shall I go from Your presence?" Paul assured us that "God is not far from every one of us, for in God we thrive and progress and have our existence." Each one of us must come to the realization that God is always present yet we continue to cry out like Jacob, "Surely the Lord is in this place; and I knew it not!"

The presence and manifestation of God are different. God is continually present even when we are not aware of His presence. God is made manifest showing us the Father, the Son and the Holy Spirit when we become totally aware of and surrender to His presence. The manifest presence of God allows the believer to exhibit the radiant power of God in great exploits. Their countenance will shine with the light of God's glory as Moses' did when they encounter God face to face.

We are successful in our pursuit to know God simply because His glorious manifested presence overshadows us. God is nearer than our breath and every concealed thought. To know God one must first hunger for His presence and then seek His face. Ask God to heal the blind eyes so they see and the deaf ears so they hear the still small whispers of His voice. When we see God's hand move and we hear His voice speaking to us we are able to break out of the timidity that demands conformity to the world. Stand up, trust and obey, seek His face and shout

God's grace from the roof tops. We are created in God's image. We have the ability to know Him if we will respond to the leading of the Holy Spirit in faith, love and practice. "But I will surely hide My face, stay out of their lives, look the other way and refuse to help them in that day because of all the evil which they have done, for they have chosen to rebel, they have turned upside down and worship other gods." (Deuteronomy 31:18 Author's paraphrase)

The Hebrew word cathar (saw-thar') means to hide or draw away, shelter, and conceal, to protect or keep secret, to retreat from being intimate. We are surrounded by an evil, rebellious generation that praises evil calling it good.

Children love to play 'hide-and-seek' as long as they are sought and found. How quickly this childhood game could turn bad insuring the child would experience feelings of rejection and abandonment if the hidden one was not hunted. Imagine being concealed in your hiding place for hours with no motion of relief. Contemplate the pain of discovering you were not desired enough to be sought out but were easily forgotten while the supposed suitors entertained themselves with some other lesser focus.

God has hidden His beautiful face and Shekinah glory in darkness, but very few seek to find Him. When we place our trust in anything other than God, we abandon God in His secret hiding place as a rejected lover. When we miss God's abiding presence we frantically begin our search for Him again. David said it best, "God, when you show me favor I am strong and fortified like a mountain. But, when You hide Your face from me I am suddenly struck with terror." (Psalms 30:8 Author's Paraphrase)

When we neglect seeking God, we reject God and the secrets He longs to share with us. God remains hidden from us to weep and grieve as Joseph had to retreat from the presence of his brothers to release the grief he felt from their betrayal. God hides from us when we break His heart until we repent and seek His face again.

Chapter 9
Creative Imagination

If we love Jesus and keep God's Word in our hearts, we will be filled with joy and our lives will reflect Jesus. We are called to be messengers of God's glory and salvation. Glory means we have a God given ability to shine God's light and presence in the world while resonating with a heavenly sound. God draws us to Himself and His angels keep us from evil. This is reflected in the beautiful prayer of (John 17). Jesus prayed as He raised His eyes to heaven, "Father, it is time to display the glory You gave me as Your only Son." You sent Me to the earthly realm, so that man may have eternal life and know You as the one true God. You are glorified in My obedience. Father as I glorify You, let Me soak in the radiant splendor of Your presence surrounding Me. I have magnified Your greatness to those you have given Me because they first belonged to You. They know the revelation knowledge I have and the message I preach came from You. Those You gave Me believe I am sent by You. I pray that My life will be displayed in the people You gave Me. You have given Me all things. What I have is from You and belongs to You. When I return to heaven those You have given Me will remain here in the world. I will not be able to guard them the way I have here on earth. Father I ask that You guard their lives. Draw them to Yourself so they will be one heart and mind with Us. I ask that You complete their joy, make them holy, consecrated with the truth of Your word. They have not joined with the ways of the world, so they are not defined by the world. The world hates them. I am not asking You to take them out of the world but to guard them from the Evil one. Just as You sent Me into the world with a message of truth, I now send them into the world with the same message. I am praying for them to be successful in their mission and witness of Me. I am also praying for those that will hear the message of salvation and believe in Me. I desire that they become one heart and mind with

Us, as You and I are one. I have given them the same glory You gave Me to unify them with Us. I am in them and You are in Me. I pray You help them mature into this oneness, that a godless world will have evidence that I was sent by God to love them in the same way You love Me. I want those You have given Me to love to always be with Me where I am. I want those who love Me to see My glory and the splendor You dwell in. Father You loved Me before the world was formed out of nothing but Your spoken words. The world does not know You, but I know and love You. The disciples You have given Me know that You sent Me because I have made You real to them. I will continue to show You and make You known to them so Your love for Me might be in them as I am already in them. (Author's paraphrase)

The eyes of the Lord are searching for those whose hearts are completely His. When God catches our attention and we spotlight Him, He will show Himself strong on our behalf. God did not create us just to maintain status quo, but to regulate earthly matters in time through His power. If you are merely maintaining, you continue in the same position or miserable state of existence without allowing change. Our words and actions create situations. In order to grow, we must embrace change to effectively develop and mature as a spirit being, rather than being ruled and guided by our carnal nature. Our dreams will give us insight into the areas we still need to cultivate in order to achieve our utmost potential and highest degree of success in God.

The life we live on earth is our training ground, a boot camp if you will, for ruling and reigning with Him in heaven. God created us in His divine image; so we possess the power to create. The decisions we make, the places we go, the things we say create images in our subconscious. First, we think a thought; then we rehearse it until it begins to formulate an image. Finally, our words speak things into existence and our actions set dynamics into motion. We are to present and display the kingdom of God that dwells within us, releasing it in powerful demonstrations. We are not called to simply exist, but to be conduits that manifest a flow of God's presence and power onto every scene and into every circumstance.

The eternal souls God created cannot be destroyed by man or "uncreated" by the enemy of our souls. Every person is an eternal being that is required to choose to love God who created them or to reject the greatest gift of all, eternal life through the salvation of Jesus. The human soul will remain forever. The question is where will that soul take up its unending residence; a glorious heaven, dwelling in peace with our Creator, God, and His angelic host or in the unprotected, dark and tormenting depths of a hell created for Satan and his demons, who abhor mankind?

Seeing Jesus

Have you been searching for the face of the invisible? Do you want to see Jesus during your life time? He promised us that He would come to us and that we would see Him (John 14:18–31). Or have you been taught that the only time you can see Jesus is when you die and go to heaven? Seeing Jesus is easier than you think! You have access to more than you can imagine! To see the beautiful face of Jesus, God's only beloved Son is the desire of every believer.

As a young woman I saw the handsome face of Jesus in a vision. During a time of prayer and peaceful reflection, Jesus came walking up to me with His arms spread wide. He stood before me with open arms that drew me to His heart. He was so real I reached out to touch Him. He was radiant, playful and charming. Pure joy, love and light flowed from His being. Jesus' olive skin was beautiful despite the scars and marks He still bore from the cruel disfiguring He endured at the crucifixion. His wavy hair was a thick golden brown that reflected the sun's blonde highlights. The smile on His lips was full, gentle, warm and inviting. His teeth were white against the frame of His beard. He was all together lovely. But the feature that stood out the most was His amazingly transparent blue eyes that twinkled with tranquil love. Their blue color reminded me of the smooth Crystal Sea that is before His throne in heaven. Never had I felt such love and acceptance in an embrace. When He appeared it was as if no one else existed in the prayer room. Everything faded until all I could see, hear or think about was Jesus. He was my focus and to my delight I was His. I fell totally in love with Jesus that day so that He is the only One my heart still longs for. Whenever I desire to see Him I just step back into that visionary experience to feel His loving presence. His loving gaze brought healing to my soul. You can receive healing too, if you will but see Jesus with open vision.

Let me teach you how to manifest Jesus in a way you can see Him.

First, turn off all noisy distractions like radio, telephones, televisions, dishwashers and the like. Go to a quiet place in your home, office, the woods, a park or garden, any place where you can get comfortable and relax (Mark 6:31, Song of Songs 4:16; 6:2, 7:11). Once and for all, rid yourself of all discouragement and thoughts of failure. Let go of the past. Take a deep breath and breathe out all worry, doubt, fear and unbelief. Set a peaceful atmosphere that will welcome His presence. Command your mind, spirit and body to come into alignment with the peace of heaven. Prepare yourself by taking a bath. Anoint yourself with DREAM ENCOUNTER anointing oil. Pray, repent and ask God to remove all your sin. Sing, adore and worship Jesus. We enter His gates with thanksgiving and into

His courts with praise. Bless the name of Jesus and tell the Lord of His exceeding greatness (Psalms 95:2, Psalms 100:4–5). Sit or lie down (Psalms 4:3–5, 8, Psalms 23:2–3). Now, cause your soul to wait in silence for God alone (Psalms 62:5–8). Take a few deep breaths to clear your head of all random thoughts. Ask the presence of the Holy Spirit to come and envelop you.

Choose to center in and intentionally focus on wanting to see the beautiful face of Jesus. Begin to thank Jesus for who He is. Express to Him what He means to you. Concentrate on how much you love Jesus. Let your love rise up until it fills your body. Now let your love come out of your body until it surrounds you like a golden glory cloud (Acts 5:15, Psalms 68:13).

Next, simply ask Jesus to manifest His love and presence (Genesis 12:7, Genesis 35:9, Exodus 3:2, 1Kings 3:5, Jeremiah 31:3). Rest and breathe deeply, relax and allow the peace that passes all understanding to come upon you (Philippians 4:7). Imagine a brilliant blue stream of radiant light coming down mixing into your golden love cloud (John 7:38). Let the Father of Lights surround you with His truth, every good thing and every perfect gift from above (James 1:17). Ask the Holy Spirit to activate your spiritual senses. Look with your spirit eyes to see, feel His company, and sense the light of God coming upon you. Ask for God's light and presence to enlarge and increase in intensity (2Thessalonias 1:3). The Holy Spirit will overshadow you. He will flow upon and in you (Luke 1:35). Embrace His anointing. Let the Holy Spirit shine forth in and from you as a radiating power field of love that will energize your life (1 Corinthians 13:13). The Holy Spirit will help you manifest your full potential by believing everything is possible with God (Mark 9:23, Mark 10:27).

Jesus' love and positive power force goes into space, time and eternity to create what is needed. Let Jesus be what you need Him to be in your life. The presence of Jesus in your life will cause people to manifest good thoughts and generate affirmative intensions toward you (Proverbs 16:7). Expect your circumstances to change for the better (Jeremiah 29:11–14). Do not allow your focus to change in order to look for verification, faith is the evidence of things hoped for while yet unseen (Hebrews 1:1–3). When you focus on God and the presence of the Holy Spirit His lively ambiance removes another veil from your face so you are able to see a new realm created in the Spirit(2 Corinthians 3:16). A maintained focus on God's presence will form a path of least resistance. This creates an open door for your future to come into the now (John 8:28–30, Luke 12:36–40, Luke13:24, Luke 10:1–5). See Jesus as the only true spiritual door that gives access to the Father; linger in His presence (Psalms 84:10). Visualize His face. Gaze into His crystal blue eyes of love (Revelation 2:18b). Look at His nail scared hands and feet. Embrace His body, feel His gentle touch, kisses and breath upon your face (Isaiah

5:1). Sense His light and loving warmth surrounding you. Hear Him speaking loving words of wisdom to you in the moment of now.

The realm of the Spirit operates with mathematical exactness. Realize that your love and desire to see Jesus activated the spiritual law of attraction (1Corinthians 15:33). Jesus was able to manifest to you at the degree of your love and the measure of faith you released toward Him (Isaiah 5:13, Hosea 4:6). Whatever quantity of faith you send out will find its match and draw it to you right now (Matthew 7). What you sow you will reap (Galatians 6:7–10). Things in the Spirit realm are already; so you do not have to look for them, hope or wish, just be, see, hear, feel and know.

Enjoy the realization of your intention of seeing Jesus manifested before you. Begin to give thanks and rejoice that your prayer has been answered (Joshua 23:14). While the Spirit of the Lord is present, position yourself to receive a message from the Spirit of God within you (1 Samuel 16:13). Listen for the still small voice of the Holy Spirit (John 10:3–5, John 5:25–32). Your spirit man is the largest part of you because it can grow and increase beyond measure (Acts 5:15, Luke 9:29–36).

Let your spirit follow the lead of the Holy Spirit. He will lead and guide you toward discovering all truth (Isaiah 42:16, John 16:13–16). Observe every thought, idea, and action casting down every vain imagination that tries to exalt itself above the knowledge of God (2 Corinthians 10:5). What small steps or major changes do you need to take to bring forth your desire into this natural realm? (Revelation 2:5–7) Faith in the Holy Spirit will link you to the detailed process that will cause people to enter your circle of influence who can teach how to draw on more of God's presence (Matthew 10:24–28).

It is important that you relinquish the reigns of control to the Holy Spirit. God will bring you the highest possible answer to the prayers you have asked (Isaiah 55:8–9). If one opportunity passes away, another better one will manifest shortly. When you walk up right nothing good will be withheld from you (Psalms 84:11). Everything will be given to you when you ask for it in the nature of God, in faith believing. Allow a measure of greater faith to be attracted into your life (Matthew 8:10–13).

How do you feel now that you have what you want? Get excited, rejoice, praise and give thanks (1 Chronicles 16:8–36, Psalms 107) That which we seek, the kingdom of God, is seeking us (Matthew 6:33, Matthew 7:7, Deuteronomy 4:29–40) Do not try to figure out how things happen because that will pull you out of the spirit realm into the carnal realm of reason and intellectual understanding. Stay focused on your heart's desire; the spirit part of you knows how spiritual things happen. Learning to accept Spirit to spirit communications will bring forth eternal results. Relax and let God bring forth something better than you can imagine (Ephesians 2:20). He desires to do exceedingly; abundantly above all we can ask or think! Simply rejoice and be thankful for God, who grants you eternal life and salvation through Jesus, has manifested Himself to you.

Chapter 10
Visions & Spiritual Perception

God did, still does and always will appear to men, women and children in various forms and manifestations. We are successful in our pursuit of God because He desires to make Himself known to man.

As a true lady must wait for romantic pursuit; so the Holy Spirit waits for our desire for Him to grow until we pursue His beautiful face with our whole heart. We behold the invisible God face to face in perfect consciousness when we live and breathe in holy desperation of His undying presence. Each morning our soul thirst for God, we gaze into His beholding face as our thankful prayers ascend into His presence. Once we see the exquisiteness of the Lord, we will reveal Jesus to the masses instead of offering a seeker friendly gospel that is absent of His presence. People will run to God, instead of running from Him, when we present His grandeur properly.

Paul, the Apostle, like John the Revelator, discovered spiritual gateways that translated him into the heavenly realms. Paul entered heavenly places; so it is also possible for us. An expectant faith, activated through the avenues of dreams, visions, prayer, reflection and meditation, praise, and worship, open heavenly doors.

In (2 Corinthians 12:1–4), Paul spoke of receiving revelatory visions from the Lord. God is incomprehensible. Yet, if we do not lift our voices in praise and adoration the very stones will cry out to declare His greatness. So how do we describe the visions we behold in another dimension that we only visit for moments at a time? When we are in the presence of a holy God we are overwhelmed with His love, yet silence prevails. How can a mere man describe the majesty of our God? What man knows the things of God? Paul assured the Athenians "God is not far from each one of us; it is through Him that we are able to live, move, be who we are and exist, as some of your own poets have stated, 'For we also are His children, we come from Him.'" (Acts 17:27–28 Authors' paraphrase)

Prophets encourage us to press past our natural limitations to pursue the indescribable majesty of our unspeakable God. Paul did not know whether he was in the body or out of the body when he was caught up into the "third heaven." He experienced "inexpressible things that man is not permitted to speak," as they can only be accurately communicated through experience. Things that take place in heaven are too wonderful for man. They are past our ability to bring a total comprehension into the earthly realms of existence. It was impossible to accurately communicate what he heard because the frequencies of heaven far exceed those of earth. Paul saw colors that surpass the limited light spectrums present in this world. Things experienced in the heavenly realms exceed man's immature understanding and childish vocabulary is insufficient to grasp and correctly communicate the spectacular wonders of heaven. Jesus when trying to communicate heavenly things used comparative words such as the kingdom of heaven is like or as.

How can our spirit conceive eternity and contemplate the greatness of an infinite God? The most eloquent human speech does not have the ability to give expressions that equal His boundless grandeur. God is complete within Himself. God spoke, and it was done; He commanded, and it stood fast, the moment God speaks things happen and come to completion. The living breath of His creative Words brought life into a clay existence; His powerful voice brought chaos into order, framed the world and formed the whole universe commanding darkness into light. His presence brings peace beyond our understanding. That is why Paul cried out, "That I might know Him!"

Our temporal minds sink into silence, they are overwhelmed when we attempt to place articulate meaning to the heavenly visions we encounter. We struggle to know the splendor of God in spiritual reality and interpretations of truth when previously we had only known of Him by the hearing of the Word or legends communicated to us by the great cloud of witnesses who have gone before. Our heart bows in awe and radiant wonder of His majestic, expansive being, when we are finally acquainted to Him. We are consumed with fearful wonder gasping, "Oh! How great is our God!" How can words describe something so glorious or someone so brilliant when we have never previously beheld the glorious presence of this magnitude? Our imaginations are creative but without an accurate knowledge of God how do we define what or who we are seeing? A. W. Tozer said, "The effort of inspired men to express the ineffable has placed a great strain upon both thought and language in the Holy Scriptures. These being often a revelation of a world above nature, and the minds for which they were written being a part of nature, the writers are compelled to use a great many "like" words to make themselves understood."[6] A. W. Tozer "The Knowledge of the Holy" (Page 6-7 published Harper Collins Publishers, 10 East 53rd Street, New York 1002, copyright 1961).

In times of trouble King David's heart whispered for him to, "Search for the face of God!" David's whole being responded in pursuit of God in humble prayer, "God Your sovereign presence has always been here for me, do not hide, or turn Your back from me now, 'My heart is seeking Your face!' "Your Spirit is current everywhere I go. I am always in Your affectionate watch. Even if I flew on the golden wings of the dawn to the farthest horizon, there I will find Your adoring gaze." David's pursuit of God was successful because God desired to be found of him. God also desires to be found of us. We will find God when we search for Him with all our heart. David perceived that God had given him the kingdom as the King of Israel. When we find His presence our perception is opened to know God's present will for us.

The religion of man is cold and complacent, stiff-necked and rebellious to the ways of God. Complacency is the enemy of spiritual hunger for it robs us of all desire. Without a desperate desire to know God, there will be no manifestation of God. When God appears we learn to love because God first loved us. When we love God passionately with our whole heart, barriers are removed and the distance of eternity fades away.

Spiritual Perception

Perception in the spiritual realm gives a person the instinctive capacity to sense spiritual beings, insights, feelings or intuitions, giftings, anointings and mantles. Perception is engaging in the intuitive ability to discern thoughts, to apprehend an impression with the mind. Spiritual perception enables us to recognize a sensible object or visionary image that is being formed in the mind's eye with one or more of the five senses. Perception facilitates the knowledge of a basic component in the formation of a concept that is gained by acknowledging that which is present, appreciable, and capable of being noticed, or detected. Perception is marked by acquiring understanding, wisdom, or discernment.

Perception is the way one sees things. Perception means to behold, to consider what one saw, or look, to see a mark, to provide vision, to see as a seer foresees the future, to gaze, to experience or meet a spiritual being, to discern how to gain counsel from the images, gifts, anointings or angelic messengers or heavenly beings that appear.

Perception is the recognition and interpretation of sensory stimuli based chiefly on the memory attaining access, and awareness or understanding of sensory information, receiving, and collecting spiritual data. It is the action of taking possession of, or the apprehension with ones' mind or senses. Input comes through our (senses), while processing takes place in the (brain), and the output come through a physical (action) with our body releasing the spiritual manifestation. Faith without works is dead!

To live in the spiritual realm of perception we must learn to be at peace in the silence of God discerning how to rest in, and wait on the Lord. We discover how to intently listen, to confidently follow, and respond appropriately to the leading of the Holy Spirit when He draws us out of the soul realm into the vast depths of His Spirit. Each time we encounter God's eternality He creates an open gate for us to access, a new precedent is formed, and an eternal unchanging principle of faith is ignited. When God allows us to encounter Him in a new way He always lays a distinct path so we can return there to visit again and again as we follow His pattern.

At first, intimacy with God causes us to be insecure until we learn to invite God's strength to overshadow our weaknesses. When we develop our trust in God's great love and mercy towards us, we become vulnerable in the presence of God. As Isaiah looked on an open heaven, he said, "Woe is me; I am a man of unclean lips." The Seraphim flew to cleanse Isaiah's lips with fire from heaven's altar enabling Isaiah to join in the dialogue of heaven stating, "Here am I Lord send me!" Isaiah went through the purification process while he was standing on earth observing and hearing heavenly things in order to become a sent one.

Every intimate God encounter has a dimension of delightful joy as we discover the mysteries of God and an element of suffering and pain when we recognize our great lack and sinfulness. We need both dimensions in order to enter into the kingdom of God. Our fears and weakness are revealed, so that we can repent, ask God's help and discover how to allow the Lord to be strong on our behalf. Total surrender of our will in worship to God releases the revelation we need to achieve our destiny. The measure of growth we experience depends on our submission to the process of understanding God's manifest presence and where we are in the succession of concealed perception.

Samuel went through a developmental process of spiritual training that ushered in a new order of faith. The young child Samuel both heard his call spoken by the Living Word of God; and Samuel both saw and felt the Lord appear before him in vision form. The Lord called, came, and stood before Samuel. The boy grew in perception because the Lord was with him. None of Samuel's words fell to the ground because he heard God's words with a comprehensible accuracy (1 Samuel

3:10). Just as it was true for Samuel, God promises us, "I will never leave you or forsake you!" Jesus went to the Father and asked Him to provide the Holy Spirit as a friend and comforter so that we would always have Him with us. This eternal friend is the Spirit of Truth. The world can not embrace Him because they do not have spiritual eyes to see Him, and they do not know what to look for. But we know the Spirit of Truth because He stays with us and resides within our very being (John 14:16–17).

Stephen was full of faith, grace, and power to perform miracles. The jealous religious leaders were void of power so they threw stones that crushed Stephen's bones and tore his flesh. In the midst of persecution and his impending death Stephen fixed his eyes on an open door in heaven and saw Jesus proudly stand to usher him into eternity.

Gideon perceived the angel of the Lord who consumed his offering, then vanished from Gideon's sight. The angel had stepped back into the coexistent spiritual realm disappearing from Gideon's physical view. Gideon feared for his life because he had seen the Lord face to face! Although the angel was now concealed from Gideon's sight… he was still very present, and continued to speak comfort to Gideon…saying, "Peace be to you, do not fear, you shall not die!"

The Spirit of the Lord directed Phillip away from the crowds, onto a deserted road to minister to one Eunuch. Then the Spirit of the Lord snatched Phillip away to another city in a spiritual transportation experience. Transportation is when the Spirit of the Lord picks a person or physical object up and carries it to a new geographic location in a moment of time.

All of these men of God knew how to go in and out of the heavenly presence of the Lord. We were created to daily encounter the God who created the endless expanse of the universe, yet still tenderly holds each of us having etched us on the palms of His loving hands. We are designed to walk and talk with the Divine, to feel the breath of the Holy Spirit, and the brush of angels wings upon our faces. Why then are we content to settle for the visible, material realm of decay when we were created to navigate the corridors of glory? Could it be because we do not understand or cooperate with the process God uses to transform us into the ministers of fire?

God introduced Himself to Moses in the wilderness at the Burning Bush encounter. Years later, God stood and revealed Himself to Moses in a cloud of glory proclaiming His names, character, and nature until Moses' face shone with God's transcendent light. When Moses caught a small glimpse of God's goodness and favor he asked to see His glory. After Moses experienced a touch of the glory he prayed for God's continual presence. Moses did not want to move from the presence of God but cried out to know Him from glory to glory. We should embrace Moses' process and develop an unsatisfied hunger for more of God.

The fire of God burns away impurities so that we can retreat into the solitary confinement of God's heart where He romances and communes with us without any distractions in the secret place. When we are totally immersed in God's love and powerful presence our spirits will thrive and expand past physical limitations.

Relating to God in the Desert

The desert is the place of one on one grace where we personally encounter God's passionate love and the treasures hidden in darkness come to light. "I will give you the treasures of darkness and hidden wealth of secret places; so that you may know that it is I, The Lord, the God of Israel, who calls you by your name" (Isaiah 45:3). We become fruitful after a season in the wilderness with God the Lover of our soul. "Therefore, behold, I will allure her, bring her into the wilderness and speak kindly to her." "Then I will give her vineyards from there, and the valley of Achor as a door of hope. And she will sing there as in the days of her youth, as in the day when she came up from the land of Egypt" (Hosea 2:14–15).

To truly know God, we will experience Him in many dimensions; of hiddenness and manifestation. Moses wanted to know God's ways and see God's glory. God gently tucked Moses away in the cleft of the rock. His hand pressed Moses until he took on and conformed to the image of Jesus the Rock. God hid Moses in Jesus, the Rock. Then God covered Moses with His hand to protect his life as God's goodness passed by. God manifested Himself to Moses in a burning bush, in a cloud by day, and as a pillar of fire by night. Moses knew God as a friend, lover, confidant, deliverer, healer, redeemer and wilderness provider. Is it possible, that if Moses had perceived God's timing and plan of deliverance correctly, he could have completed his training and preparation process in the king's palace instead of having been exiled, driven into the desert wilderness after he took matters into his own hands and murdered an Egyptian? (Esther was taken from her home and Uncle to be groomed in the palace to save her nation from destruction.) People like Joseph and Daniel served by interpreting dreams in the Kings courts. Those who are called to deliver a nation are high profile people who are groomed in the judicial realms of government.

With Joshua God came as the Angel of the Lord, the Captain of the Host. For Daniel He was the Fourth man in the fire. Jesus came in His post resurrection transfigured form with the disciples on the Mount. Today the God who created the universe invades our hearts to reveal Himself to us through dreams and visions that restore our souls. Every successful man and woman of God has gone through the boot camp of God. The wilderness empowers each of us to use spiritual weapons so we can disciple others in their unique giftings and destiny.

Elijah stood before the Lord of host with a spiritual receptivity that was profound. Receptivity means that the mind is qualified, ready, and willing to embrace impressions or ideas that enhance the memory. "A person is shown only what is reflected in his own mind." So the renewing of the mind by the washing of God's Word becomes paramount in our lives. Jesus is the Living Word, He is before all things, and in Him all things hold together. Both heaven and earth will eventually pass away but the Word of God is eternal it will never pass away. Elijah mentored and passed his qualifications and aware attitude onto Elisha who further cultivated his skills of perception in order to carry God's perspectives until he was able to receive twice the spirit of Elijah. Elisha's prayer urged his spiritually blind servant to look towards God's light so the veil could be removed from his eyes. When the servant lifted his fearful gaze heavenward his natural eyes were opened to see the angelic host encamped around about them.

Solomon received God's gift of wisdom in a dream. He exclaimed, "O God of glory who dwells above the heavens; will You really dwell on the earth? Why the whole sky, heaven and the highest heaven cannot contain You, so how much less this house which I have built!" (1 Kings 8:27–28 Authors' Paraphrase) Solomon's words were the calculations of sound wisdom and ardent study. God's Words are the blessed essence of truth. When God whispers the whole world listens to gain wisdom.

Jesus, God's only Son, is our moral compass. He directs us into spiritual places where everything depends upon us yielding to the Holy Spirit's will and being obedient in a harmonious relationship with God. God's greatest desire is for us to know and continually experience Him. He wants to be our all in all obsession, our great inheritance, and supreme part in life.

Visitation

In times of visitation God teaches us what we do not know; so we can adjust our positional gaze to recognize the presence of God. If God is here among us, living in us, and everywhere around us, we are dislocated like Jacob, who after gazing upon Jesus in a vision cried out, "Surely God is in this place; and I knew it not!" We must use our limited knowledge and spiritual perception to transport us past the mundane and recognizable into the vast spiritual dimensions of the unknown expanses of God.

Manifestation

In times of manifestation, the presence of Jesus is with us, so there are no deep secrets shared, because our understanding is limited. Then Jesus took the twelve aside and said to them, "Behold, we are going up to Jerusalem, and all things which are written through the prophets about the Son of Man will be accomplished. "For He will be handed over to the Gentiles, and will be mocked and mistreated and spit upon, and after they have scourged Him, they will kill Him; and the third day He will rise again." But the disciples understood none of these things, and the meaning of this statement was hidden from them, and they did not comprehend the things that were said. (Luke 18:31–34) Hidden manna is released after we have overcome trials and testings by learning to live in the secret place where our internal man is developed through embracing serenity.

The being of God's essence is always present but we are not always able to perceive Him. God only manifest when we wholly connect to and surrender to, the will of His existence, with our faith knowing and recognizing the radiant, beautiful face of His presence. Decide to always place the Lord's face before your eyes and with skilled determination forever keep Him the focus of your heart. "But to this day whenever Moses is read, a veil lies over their heart; but whenever a person turns to the Lord, the veil is taken away. Now the Lord is the Spirit, and where the Spirit of the Lord is, there is liberty. But we all, with unveiled face, beholding as in a mirror the glory of the Lord, are being transformed into the same image from glory to glory, just as from the Lord, the Spirit" (2 Corinthians 3:15–18).

Salvation brings the restoration of a divine connection and perfect alignment between God and man. We must be totally preoccupied with our love and adoration of the Triune God for who He is, not for the things He does. God is the self-existent Creator of the ever expanding universe, in whom all things come into existence for His pleasure, in Him they continue living and have their being. To know Him is to be possessed with a hunger and thirst for more God consciousness, to cry out, "Give me all of Thee; for there is nothing more, there is nothing else, but You oh God!"

Jesus the Healer

Jesus was so sensitive to the anointing that He perceived power leaving His body when faith touched His clothes…when Jesus inquired of the disciples "Who touched Me?" They responded, "Master, the multitudes throng and press You, and You say, "Who touched Me?" But Jesus said, "Somebody touched Me with faith, for I perceived power going out from Me." Now when the woman with an issue of blood saw that she was not hidden, she came trembling; and falling down before Him, she declared to Him in the presence of all the people the reason she had touched Him and how she was healed immediately. And Jesus said to her, "Daughter, be of good cheer; your faith has made you well. Go in peace" (Luke 8:45–48).

Wicked Religious Hearts

Jesus perceived wickedness that was hidden within the hearts of the Pharisees and Herodians. "Teacher, we know that You are truthful and teach the way of God in truth, and defer to no one; for You are not partial to any." "Tell us then, what do You think? Is it lawful to give a poll-tax to Caesar, or not?" But Jesus perceived their malice, and said, "Why do you test Me, you hypocrites? Show Me the tax money." So they brought Him a denarius. And He said to them, "Whose image and inscription is this?" They said to Him, "Caesar's." And He said to them, "Render therefore to Caesar the things that are Caesar's, and to God the things that are God's." When they had heard these words, they marveled, and left Him and went their way (Matthew 22:18–22).

A large crowd gathered within and without the house to hear Jesus speak. While Jesus was teaching, four men carried a paralyzed man to see Him. Because the house was overflowing with people they carried him to the roof above Jesus. They made a hole then lowered the paralyzed man on his mat. When Jesus saw the faith that exuded from them, he said to the paralyzed man, "Young man, your sins are forgiven."

The teachers of the law were there thinking to themselves and reasoning within their hearts "Why does Jesus say things to insult God? No one but God can forgive sins." Jesus immediately perceived and knew in the spirit what these teachers of the law were thinking. So he asked them, "Why do you have these questions in your minds? The Son of Man has power on earth to forgive sins. But how can I prove this to you? You are thinking it was easy for me to say to the crippled man, 'Your sins are forgiven.' But, there's no proof it really happened. But on the contrary if I say to the man, 'Be healed! Stand up! Take your mat and walk?' Then you will be able to see that I really have the power to forgive sins and to heal." So Jesus said to the paralyzed man, "I tell you, stand up. Take your mat and go home" (Mark 2:2–11).

Jesus still heals today. Recently, I met an atheist at a bike park in Texas. He was celebrating his sixtieth birthday. As I listened to all the reasons he did not believe that Jesus was real I discovered he had torn ligaments in his shoulder. I boldly announced that Jesus wanted to give him a birthday present. What? He responded. I said, "Jesus wants to prove He is real and that He loves you by healing your torn ligaments." He responded with yea right! So I gently laid hands on him and prayed, "Jesus heal his shoulder." His face looked surprised as he began to move his shoulder around and found that he was now pain free. He dropped to the ground and did several push ups still no pain. Jesus had healed him. "Ok you are healed! Now that you know Jesus is real there is no reason why you should not accept Him as your Lord and Savior. Pray this prayer with me." "Jesus, I believe you are real. I am a sinner. I ask that you forgive me of all my sins. I believe that you died for my sins to cleanse me from all wrong. Please save my soul. Jesus, I receive you as my Lord and Savior. Come into my heart to stay." Immediately his countenance changed to one of light.

As we walked towards the parking lot he shared that one of his legs was shorter than the other. So I asked him to sit down on the curb. I knelt down and grabbed both of his ankles to see which leg was longer. His right leg was about four inches shorter than his left leg. I was about to pray for God to heal him when I heard the Holy Spirit say, "No! Do not pray for him." So I froze and waited not sure what to do next. Then I heard the Holy Spirit say, "I want him to ask me to heal his leg." What a relief. This man had been save all of two minutes and was getting ready to do a miracle of healing on his own body. I looked up and said, "The Holy Spirit wants you to pray and ask Jesus to heal your leg." "How do I do that he asked?" I answered, "Simple say, "Jesus please grow my leg out!" He assumed the prayer position with his hands tucked and folded under his chin. He had both eyes closed but suddenly he opened one eye in expectation of seeing his leg grow out. He whispered, "Jesus grow my leg out!" Instantly, his right leg grew out four inches to match his left leg. After seeing his miracle take place he remained seated with both hands covering his face. As the anointing continued to flood his body his face turned red and he broke a sweat. After a few silent moments he stood up and with tears streaming down his face he gave a real living God thanks for saving and healing him on his birthday.

The powers that Jesus possessed when He was on earth came through the intimate times He sought His Father in prayer; not because He was the Son of God. He had laid aside His divinity to walk the earth as a man. Jesus perceived that the people were about to come and take Him by force to make Him their king (John 6:15). Jesus sent the crowd away, made the disciples get into the boat and go ahead of Him to the other side, while He departed again to the mountain to be alone and pray. When Jesus went up the mountain He did not know how to walk on water. But after He sought His Father for the wisdom of how to rejoin His disciples on the water, He was granted the knowledge of how to defy natural laws of gravity. When walking on water became necessary the mystery was revealed to Jesus during His prayer watch at night.

Walk on the Water

The disciples' boat was battered by the winds and waves a great distance from shore. Jesus came to the disciples walking on the sea, during the fourth watch of the night. When the disciples saw Jesus walking on the sea, they falsely perceived Him as a ghost. They cried out in fear utterly terrified. Immediately Jesus spoke peace to them, saying, "Take courage, it is I; do not be afraid." Peter answered Jesus, "Lord, if it is You, command me to come to You on the water." And Jesus said, "Come!" Peter stepped out of the boat, and walked toward Jesus on the water Matthew (14:22–30). Peter was the only one who was willing to take a chance and change the ghostly perception he held of Jesus. Jesus desired that all of the disciples embraced a faith filled perception of Him, take a chance, get out of the boat and walk with Him on the water. God wants to empower us to stretch the limits of our spiritual and physical comfort zones. It is time to take a risk. Get out of the confines of our safe boats, defy the laws of nature, do creative miracles and walk on water.

We are not like minded with God in our natural finite state. God does not change; so we must renew our mind with His Word so that we can align ourselves with His divine nature. We understand or perceive thing in a linear fashion. We start at the beginning (A) and finish at (Z) with a specific goal in mind. We measure everything by the time it will take us to produce something, complete a task, or reach a deadline. We are process and time oriented. We move from a departure point advancing with a specific destination in mind. God's goal in teaching us spiritual perception is for us to learn to enjoy every aspect of the journey we take while developing our relationship with Him. But, we are so linear in our thinking we are only concerned with reaching our destiny so we can manifest His power.

God is eternal, proceeding, instantaneous, and cyclical. God does not take short cuts or move in straight lines He is always ascending. God functions and exists outside of space and time. God is the Alpha and Omega, the beginning and the end all at the same time. He is the all in all; complete whole, omniscient, omnipresent, God. God measures our spiritual development by our ability to grow in faith, spiritual perception, obedience, and the understanding of His ways; not by the amount of time we have been saved.

When God imagines a happening in His heart it is already an authentic reality. When God speaks or prophesies heaven immediately performs His will to bring events into existence. The angels around God's throne cry, "Holy, holy, holy!" every time God reveals a new dimension of Himself. On earth we perceive God's presence, hear and receive God's Word, and then we begin the process of walking the promise out. God relates to us in the spirit as if the promise has already taken place. It is done, accomplished and manifested in the realm of the spirit. We see, when we believe, and by faith, we access things spoken by God to bring them into our now reality. The future becomes a now reality when we release our faith to obtain it.

The human spirit allows us to exercise intelligence, perception, and determination, to make moral choices. It enables us to exceed above the physical realm, and have dominion over, any situation or other creature in the earth realm. This intrinsic worth drives us to know our Creator as well as to know the hope of our calling and the reason we exist. The spirit is the highest function of our being. We are first and foremost spiritual beings.

It is through our spirits that we commune with the spiritual world and the God who created us. When we open our human spirits and allow the Holy Spirit to come and reside within us, we come into a divine connection and holy union with our Creator. It is through our human spirits that the Holy Spirit gives us the revelation necessary to accomplish His will and our specific purpose on the earth. This is an ongoing process, so we should expect God to commune with us daily as we diligently seek Him.

Mercy will keep our spiritual eyes open, so that we can triumph over the pointing of the finger, criticism and judgment. Mercy is the kind and compassionate treatment of others. When we walk in love, our spiritual vision and perceptions remain pure. By offering God's great gift of grace to those who harm, or persecute us, we will not only bless them, but it will also lead us to a personal victory.

The more we come to know God and His ways, the clearer our visionary sight becomes. The foggy mist that distorts our vision begins to clear and evaporate. When we don't know God, our vision is dim, like having to watch life through the reflection of a smoky mirror. Our natural perception and understanding is limited, and we only know and see in part. The closer we draw to God to discern His presence and ways, the more fully we will know God in spirit and in truth. Resting in God's glorious shadow we discover our desperate need for Him. God will manifest His being, goodness and power right before our eyes. Our vision will expand, and God's plan for our lives will come into focus and clarity.

The Visionary Seer

Seers are visionary dreamers who have the divine supernatural ability to see the future. Spiritual beings and apparitions appear to them that are normally invisible or unperceivable to others. Seers watch and reenact that which they see displayed in the spirit.

To develop one's seer's gift it is essential to access understanding in the realms of spiritual perception and revelatory vision. A vision is defined as "the faculty of sight; something that is or has been seen; an unusual capability in discernment or perception." Visions give us an unusual capability to perceive or discern through intelligent foresight; the way in which one sees, or conceives of, or perceives something that is to come in the future." Visions are mental images created by the imagination, the mystical experience of seeing spiritual beings from the supernatural realm with our spiritual or natural eyes. Visions deposit the Word of God within us to establish truths that have already transpired in the spirit realm but have not manifested in the physical realm yet. Prophesying the vision creates a doorway that allows the vision of God to become a reality. Visions reveal spiritual movement in heaven and on earth. Visions can be experienced again just by reciting the visual experience, recalling the pictures, and reliving the feelings, sensations, and emotions of the event. We can receive visions when we are awake or asleep. Revelation comes to us through our spiritual visual perception.

Seers carry the silence of God's whisper into the areas of perspective and spiritual perception. God brings a heightened sensitivity to our spiritual perceptions by aligning them with our natural senses. God wants us to be able to see Him, perceive everything about Him, to know what He is doing. We are able to participate in His grand acts and release them to manifest His greatness in ourselves and through others. God mirrors Himself in and through us as He steps out of the invisible realm into the natural realm of our reality, transforming it into the supernatural realms of the Divine.

Seers reflect the treasures of revelation to the outside world from the intimate dimensions of God Himself. "Lift up your heads, O gates, and be lifted up, O ancient doors that the King of glory may come in! Who is the King of glory? The Lord strong and mighty, The Lord mighty in battle. Lift up your heads, O gates, and lift them up, O ancient doors, that the King of glory may come in!" (Psalms 24:7–9) We contain both the physical portal and spiritual gates that allow God to enter into us from heaven to move through us on earth. Our eye gates see, the ear gates hear, and the nose gates discern, the skin gates feel and transfer His touch, and the mouth gates speak His praises, declare His truth and creative healing Word.

Seers mirror God's actions to mankind by giving them entrance or manifestation to the world, thus God's heavenly presence is established on earth. Therefore, seers communicate as extensions of God's limitlessness and His endless expansion throughout all of eternity. Seers are utilized by God to bring into existence what God brings out, displays, or reveals through the breathing in and out, of the ebb and flow of the Spirit's creativity. That which the Lord reveals is ours to receive, possess, and demonstrate in our daily lives.

Seers interact with the great cloud of witnesses, spiritual realms of heavenly creatures, beasts, lights, winds, and a host of heavenly beings, angels, messengers, and ministering spirits. Seers have developed an intimate relationship with the Lord Jesus, who is the only true gateway or door to the spiritual realm. A literal physical and spiritual restoration process takes place in the presence of God's anointing.

The primary function of seers is to see the things God shows them in the concealed realm. Seers receive revelation knowledge through the invisible angelic realms of visions, trances, and dreams. Seers are called to relate to God through the intimacy of faith, hope, and love. An atmosphere of peaceful meditation allows seers to enter into the spiritual perception of visionary sight. They are able to gaze into the invisible realms of glory and behold the beauty of the Lord, and so are you! David said it this way, "One thing I have asked from the Lord, that I shall seek: That I may dwell in the house of the Lord all the days of my life, to behold the beauty of the Lord and to meditate in His temple" (Ps.27:4). Beholding Jesus or "meditating upon His Word," is the act that brings transformation to the heart and mind. For what we behold, we become (Josh. 1:8, Rom. 12:2, and 2 Cor. 3:18). For an in depth study of the Seer please read my book, GATEWAY to the SEER REALM Look Again to See Beyond the Natural which is available at www.BarbieBreathitt.com.[7]

What do you see? God wants to change your perception. He wants to open our eyes to see so that we can know Him in a new way. God said, "Behold the former things have come to pass, I make all things new. I do a new thing, do you not perceive it?" (Isa. 42:9). His mercies are new every morning. His magnificent rising is beyond our comprehension. Since the Holy Spirit is God, He can come, and manifest anyway He desires! "Do not earnestly remember the former things neither consider the things of old," (Isaiah 43:18–19, 26). "Remember this, and be assured; recall it to mind, you transgressors." "Remember the former things long past, for I am God, and there is no other; I am God, and there is no one like Me, declaring the end from the beginning, and from ancient times things which have not been done, saying, 'My purpose will be established, and I will accomplish all My good pleasure'; (Isaiah 46:8–10). God is asking, do you not perceive the new thing; the innovative ways in which I am coming? So often we do not understand or perceive the ways and strategies of God. God's ways are beyond finding out. How does light communicate? God is light, an energy force, and a spiritual vibration that resonates at a higher frequency than our natural, physical, mental or emotional facilities can comprehend. Do we even know or understand the smallest of God's ways? Have our religious traditions locked us into a narrow scope of interaction? The holy God of heaven wants to interact with His children in every conceivable way. Moses wanted to know God's ways and His glory, (Exodus 33:18). God comes in a unique and special way through every person; but we don't recognize the various forms and expression of God when they are resident in man.

The Realm of Wisdom

Perception is a realm of wisdom where the spirit activates our senses, to perceive Jesus in His multifaceted ways. Jesus always desires to take us further. Jesus would have walked further down the Emmaus Road; past the natural darkness, into the divine supernatural manifestation of His presence instead of entering the house to rest. "By wisdom a house is built, and by understanding it is established; and by knowledge the rooms are filled with all precious and pleasant riches." (You are a spiritual HOUSE!) "A wise man is strong, and a man of knowledge increases power. For by wise guidance you will wage war, and in abundance of counselors there is victory" (Proverbs 24:3–6). The Bible further states, "For every house is built by someone, but the builder of all things is God" (Hebrews 3:4). Job asked God, "Where is wisdom found?" "God saw wisdom and declared it; He established wisdom and also searched it out. "And to man He said, 'Behold, the fear of the Lord, that is wisdom; and to depart from evil is understanding'" (Job 28:27–28). God understands wisdom's way, and He knows wisdom's place. Wisdom is found as man learns to trust God, leaning not on his own understanding but acknowledging God in all his ways. Wisdom is not found in this world. Wisdom is located between the spiritual doors and chambers of transitioning as we enter from one realm of understanding to the next higher luminal realm. "The Spirit of the Lord will rest on Him, the spirit of wisdom and understanding, the spirit of counsel and strength, the spirit of knowledge and the fear of the Lord" (Isaiah 11:2). As God releases the different aspects of His Spirit and we learn the operations of the seven spirits of God (Rev. 4:5), the reverential fear of the Lord will return and spiritual wisdom will be discovered.

Jesus is our only hope of perfection through faithfully practicing spiritual receptiveness. Without the love of Jesus, our hearts are barren clay vessels, cracked and full of want. When total surrender comes the Master Potter lovingly removes the marred surface of our disfigured lives and fills in the cracked places where we have suffered great loss. He molds and remakes us into His image perfectly shaping the clay into a beautiful vessel of honor. Unless the Master leads us step by step no one could find their way to Father God. "But solid food is for the mature, who because of practice have their senses trained to discern good and evil" (Hebrews 5:14).

Spiritual Maturity

Spiritual maturity brings us into completeness. There are three things that will lead us toward consummation or wholeness: A steady trust in God, an unswerving hope in Christ, and most of all a baptism in His extravagant fiery love! The eyes of the Lord are searching for those with a servant's heart of love so that He can support and promote them. "For the eyes of the Lord move to and fro throughout the earth that He may strongly support those whose heart is completely His..." (2 Chron.16:9). If we want God's support we must give Him our whole heart.

Spiritual maturity evolves as revelation is received during intimate seasons of fellowship in the presence of God. We move into a higher realm of existence when our minds are renewed to think and perceive events the way God does. "For My thoughts are not your thoughts, nor are your ways My ways," declares the Lord. "For as the heavens are higher than the earth, so are My ways higher than your ways and My thoughts than your thoughts. For as the rain and the snow come down from heaven, and do not return there without watering the earth and making it bear and sprout, and furnishing seed to the sower and bread to the eater; so will My word be which goes forth from My mouth; it will not return to Me empty, without accomplishing what I desire, and without succeeding in the matter for which I sent it" (Isaiah 55:8–11).

When God conceals Himself from us it is to draw us to Him in the realm of the spirit. God demonstrates His pleasure with us by enabling us to experience a season of profound discovery and breakthrough. God teaches us His ways when we are secluded in His loving embrace. These times of intimacy help us to process our disappointments and disillusionment. When our understanding is enlightened, we gain new expectations, as we submit and conform to God's higher plans. John 6: The Holy Spirit builds us up in Christ by laying a broader understanding in the foundation of the Word to establish more of the thoughts and ways of Christ in us.

When God hides Himself from us He touches our spirit in the dimensions of godly wisdom, communion, and consciousness so that we can experience His glory. "Truly, You are a God who hides Himself, O God of Israel, Savior!" (Isaiah 45:15). God is our hiding place, refuge, and high tower Psalm 91. God hides in the broad open places so we can look past the natural limitations of life, into the supernatural realms of abundance to find His presence continually surrounding us. Intimacy with God is the incubator that develops expectancy, the internal perspective of the spirit which postures us to have an intentionality of receive revelation.

God draws us into the desert to teach us His higher ways; instead of trusting our learning to the fallibility of man. God's presence always abides with us; He will never depart or abandon us. God sustains us, provides for and increases our understanding in the wilderness. "But you have an anointing from the Holy One, and you all know" (1 John 2:20).

When we exit the desert we are able to live in the spirit. There we learn to draw from the eternal well of living water. Trusting in God's peaceful embrace births perseverance; internal rest, power, and spiritual authority.

Spiritual Disciplines

Spiritual disciplines are formed in the dry desert times of life. Exclusive times of intimate communion with God's presence bring our souls into a place where we can find a peaceful delight in the Lord. We learn to accept God's sovereign will even when it conflicts with our present desire, hope or expectations. Here in His tender embrace we learn to conform to His perfect will for our lives. The mature spirit knows that God is first within us before He can flow out of us; while the soul continues to look for answers from an external source. "But whoever drinks of the water that I will give him shall never thirst; but the water that I will give him will become in him a well of water springing up to eternal life" (John 4:14).

Spiritual Enlightenment

Enlightenment comes when we are safely hidden within God. The enormity of the trials that are forged against us predicts the immensity of our calling, level of gifting and kingdom impact. Do not ask "Why" Lord? But, humbly ask, "What are You showing me in this trial? What do I need to learn?" "Help me understand so that I can change to become more like You!" David cried out, "How long, O Lord? Will You forget me forever? How long will You hide Your face from me? How long shall I take counsel in my soul, having sorrow in my heart all the day? How long will my enemy be exalted over me? Consider and answer me, O Lord my God; enlighten my eyes, or I will sleep the sleep of death, and my enemy will say, "I have overcome him, "and my adversaries will rejoice when I am shaken. But I have trusted in Your lovingkindness; my heart shall rejoice in Your salvation. I will sing to the Lord, because He has dealt bountifully with me" (Psalms 13).

Spiritual upgrades bring a divine acceleration in favor and influence through a quickening spirit because the spirit realm moves at the speed of light. Being hidden in Christ empowers us to understand the revelation we receive that takes us to the next level of maturity to touch and impact the nations for God. The enemy can not touch us when we are hidden in the secret place of God's heart. God desires to move us out of the mundane realms where we exist on a natural plane, so we can thrive planted in Him, living in a place of abundance and overflow.

Jesus was full of the Spirit when He was led by the Holy Spirit into the wilderness to be tested. (Luke 4:1) The desert teaches us to trust in God's supernatural provision. When the enemy of our soul comes to tempt us with compromise, we are able to erect and maintain a high standard of excellence. We learn the power of a humble, contrite heart as our ego decreases; God becomes magnified and more evident in our thoughts and demonstrated in our daily actions. We succeed when we totally release the ownership of every kingdom of our lives to the Holy Spirit. In becoming less, we actually become much more.

Through the wilderness process our greatest joy becomes that of being a servant to all. We discover the importance of not testing God when God is trying our hearts and testing our faithfulness to determine the measure of anointing we can carry. In surrendering our will to God's greater plans and purposes we thrive in every area of life thus rising to the top! For God's plans have always been for us to be the head and not the tail, to be above the situations of life and not beneath. In trusting His higher ways we are able to spring forth in renewed hope and divine expectation of a new day dawning. God carries the weight of the call, while we enjoy being equally yoked with Him throughout the journey of life.

The wilderness establishes a greater sense of the impossible nature of our calling so that when our doubts and fears are exposed, God can remove them to develop a greater measure of faith and trust in us. Our insecurities turn into a vulnerability that trusts in the ways of God. We learn to exchange the desperate cry of our soul's that says, "Give me strength, so I can accomplish the unobtainable." To the spirit's thankful declaration of gratitude for God choosing us in our weakness so He can manifest His strength through us.

God's Manifest Presence

The manifestations of God that demonstrates His presence are temporary. So in our humanity, we fixate on past experiences and historic moves of God. We expect God to come in the exact same way and expressions, while the grace and mercy of the living progressive Word of God is new every morning. God's manifestation involves blessing, visitation, and the outpouring of God's sovereignty as the escalating changes in the anointing of God bring an increase in revelation knowledge. These spiritual gateways of knowledge propel us into new spheres of glory that allow us to create habitations for God.

In manifestation God touches our body and soul; in the dimensions of the mind, will, and emotions. When He appears it is to transform and move us forward in our relationship with Him. He always comes to accomplish a goal or specific purpose in us.

In times of visitation, God teaches us what we do not know; so we can adjust our positional gaze to recognize the presence of God in diverse ways. Visitations come to condition and prepare us to become a place of habitation for the presence of God to indwell. God is looking for a dwelling place where He can rest His glorious head upon a body that has become His temple formed from living fiery stones that reflect His multiple facets and manifest the radiant light of His being.

God is the same to us in the secret place and in the desert because He is unchanging. When we are transformed into God's image our thoughts and ways will be unchanged by the circumstances that surround us. We will place our hope in God and will no longer be disquieted. "O God, You are my God; I shall seek You earnestly; my soul thirsts for You, my flesh yearns for You, in a dry and weary land where there is no water. Thus I have seen You in the sanctuary, to see Your power and Your glory. Because Your lovingkindness is better than life, my lips will praise You. So I will bless You as long as I live; I will lift up my hands in Your name. My soul is satisfied as with marrow and fatness, and my mouth offers praises with joyful lips. When I remember You on my bed, I meditate on You in the night watches, for You have been my help, and in the shadow of Your wings I sing for joy. My soul clings to You; Your right hand upholds me" (Psalms 63:1–8). As it was for David, so it is for us today.

The Manifestation of the Holy Spirit

The Holy Spirit is the tangible substance of God. He is the divine third person of the Trinity. Holy Spirit is the essence of God's own being and personality. All heavenly beings are composed of spiritual substance or heavenly material. God is a Spirit who transmits His living presence and abundant life-force into our minds, flesh and spirits (John 10:10).

A good example of the Holy Spirit's radiating power is at the transfiguration of Jesus. The Spirit of God came upon Jesus until His face, clothes and whole being glowed with a white, glory light as bright as the noonday sun (Matthew 17:23). Jesus demonstrated the fact that the body of man was able to both receive the Holy Spirit's indwelling presence and manifest Him through the outshining of His glory. Those who worship God must learn to worship Him in Spirit and in truth through the quickening of the Spirit of God (John 4:24). We must know God with out spirits to reveal Him in His power.

We can transmit a portion of the life-force of God's Spirit that dwells within us. The Apostle Paul contained and exuded so much of the Holy Spirit's presence that the handkerchiefs and aprons he touched became conduits that carried the anointing of God to heal the sick and deliver the insane and demon possessed. Because He is God He can manifest anyway He desires. Breath of the Spirit sends anointed prayer clothes to their partners who are sick or in need. We have received many testimonies of cancer being healed, depression and suicide leaving when people touched or wore the clothes we sent through the mail. The Apostle Peter's spirit shone out beyond him as a Holy Spirit shadow that delivered and healed the people it touched when he walked through the marketplaces and streets of his day.

Holy Spirit was demonstrative as a powerful creator in Genesis; as a pillar of fire by night and a cloud by day to protect His chosen in (Exodus 13:21–22). The Holy Spirit manifested as a dove at Jesus' baptism. The heavens opened and the audible voice of God proclaimed, "This is My beloved Son in whom I am well pleased." (Luke4:1–14). The Holy Spirit appeared as a mighty rushing wind and cloven tongues of fire that rested on people's heads empowering them for the divine supernatural (Acts2:2).

The secret to living the successful Christian life is in possessing the manifest presence of the Holy Spirit, and demonstrating the character and nature of Jesus Christ in your life. Life without the indwelling of the Holy Spirit's power wearies the flesh. It narrows Christianity to a list of commands to obediently follow but the flesh is left without the imparted power to do so.

Although Jesus is the perfect Son of God, He still had to cycle through the wilderness in order to establish His acceptance and identity in God the Father. The Holy Spirit filled Jesus and then led Him into the wilderness to be trained, tried, tested, and proved faithful. Jesus went into the wilderness in the fullness of God's favor. Jesus was not taken into the wilderness because He had done something wrong, or to be punished. God was celebrating His Son. When the testing process was completed, Jesus exited the wilderness in the overflowing power of God.

Every one of us is as close to and as full of God's presence and power as we desire to be. We will be filled to the measure that we hunger and desire to know God in His fullness. Holy Spirit covers us with His grace, so we become presentable inside and out. His forgiveness cleanses and purifies our inner life allowing us to draw nearer to cultivate the presence of God in confidence. There we receive mercy, wisdom and find grace in our time of need. God is not far-off in a distant heaven He continually resides within our spirits.

Grieving the Holy Spirit

The Holy Spirit dwells within the remolded heart of man conforming us into His image. He is closer than our concealed thoughts, our soul or the breath that we breathe. When we repent of our fascination with the visible, tangible things of this world our eyes will be opened to see God's invisible beauty from a higher vantage point. Those who do not embrace God's higher ways and thoughts find themselves with no sense of moral values or significance. They will not know the difference between right and wrong, good or evil, the holy or the profane. So calling good evil they bring a curse upon themselves and perish before their time.

Reporters notify us of calamities and disaster but they always deal with the earthly realms of worldly reasoning about racism, wars, and rumors of war, earthquakes and famine, the natural existence of things that have already been foretold. The greatest calamity of our time is that like news reporters, most religious orators or leader's have deaf ears that are closed to the still small voice of the Holy Spirit, the heavens are silent to them and as impenetrable as brass. They continue to try to know and understand God through an intellectual pursuit and have no spiritual power, only knowing God through that which is motivated by the soul. They manipulate the crowds through emotional pleas or mental gymnastics. They deal with issues of mediocrity and political compromise by using their carnal reasoning just like worldly leaders. The world is not able to discern any difference between the holy and the profane because the church has allowed the demarcation lines to become clouded and smeared.

This grieves the Holy Spirit and those whose hearts cry out for the living God to make His presence known. Where are the righteous men and women of faith who know how to ascend before the throne of God and intimately engage with the All Powerful? Is it even feasible for those who know God to share and display their pearls of wisdom and great exploits that are gained in this spiritual experience? Most of the church and the world at large does not believe a personal, tangible encounter with a living God is possible. They speak about God in general terms, but they do not know Him, or how to enter into His Spirit to obtain truth that heals and liberates. What they communicate to their audiences about God would be considered inadmissible evidence in a court of law. It would be thrown out as "hear say or second hand information." Their critical hearts and intellectual minds have not developed a spiritual depth, so they jealously drown and accuse those who have ventured into the deep places of intimacy with God; overwhelming and discrediting them as simple minded or childish, while destroying them with their religious skepticism, doubt and unbelief.

Believers must reacquaint themselves with the spiritual wisdom and true knowledge of God, which is generously only given to those who pursue God with wholehearted passion in order to regain their power and influence once again. It is of utmost importance that the whole world encounters the living powerful God. A God encounter is imperative for our continued existence and prosperity. Our blinded eyes cannot know God by external earthly pursuits that are confined to the soulish realm of the Knowledge of Good and Evil. It is the Holy Spirit who reveals Jesus, the Living Word; The Tree of Life and the deep and hidden things which are freely given to us of God.

Open Heavens

Ezekiel gazed into an open heaven. There he beheld the invisible. He saw visions of what appeared to be the enormity of God appearing in the likeness of man. God was seated on a sapphire stone throne obscured by an amber cloud of glory with a blazing fire that enfolded itself. Ezekiel struggled with the correct verbiage to describe the magnitude of what he saw as the appearance of the likeness of the glory of the Lord. When Ezekiel saw the glory, he fell upon his face. Then he heard a voice of one that spoke.

Ezekiel suggested that the heavenly creatures around the throne resembled things he had seen on earth so he tried to bring intelligibility in a natural likeness. "As for the likeness of their faces, they four had the face of a man, and the face of a lion, on the right side: and they four had the face of an ox on the left side; they four also had the face of an eagle." "As for the likeness of the living creatures, their appearance was like burning coals of fire…" (Ezekiel 1:10, 13).

When God took Ezekiel to the Valley of Dry Bones He asked, "Ezekiel, Can these bones live?" Ezekiel did not presume to know anything in the presence of an All-Knowing God. He humbly responded, "O Lord God, You alone know!" Ezekiel's heart was open and surrendered to discovering the mystery presented by God. Arrogant speech is a luxury none can afford in the presence of the Mighty. When confronted by the delight of God's presence the prophetic seer waited in silence to hear what the Lord would whisper in response.

God is the God of perfect love; but He also has feelings of anger, joy, emotional desires and disappointments, divine thoughts and attributes that cause Him to suffer and be grieved just like a person. Can we by searching, find the face of the invisible God? Once we find Him in the midst of us, can we adequately honor, love and describe His almighty perfection?

No man knows God the Father, except Jesus and to he whom Jesus chooses to reveal His Father. There is a yearning in the deepest depths of man's spirit to knowingly comprehend God. Man desires to touch God's heart, to taste His goodness and experience the incomprehensible love of the unapproachable face of God. We are helpless to know God with our mind but must transcend the mental recesses of reason to know God by faith in the Spirit of Jesus. Without a personal encounter with God His Words do not penetrate the icy soul but continue to roll off the hard heart. It takes time to cultivate the knowledge and experience of God. Faith in Christ opens the door to spiritual knowledge and the wings of love lift us up to a superior realm that empowers us to experience God's presence and taste the sweetness of God.

What do we exalt above, place our trust in, or allow taking precedence over, Gods majesty in our lives? If given a choice to receive untold riches of wealth beyond description, success and the accolades of fame, or the treasure of grace offered by the love of an invisible God, which would we choose? Will we keep our moral compass focused upon the bright and Morningstar who fights from heaven to light our way or allow the tempest storms to blow us off course until our ship wrecks upon the barren shore? Will we renounce our friends, family, and the comforts of life, along with our reputation and ambitions to remain in obscurity even if it means we must stand all alone to exalt God? We honor God by exalting and serving Him above all. The strength God gives us in return for honoring Him enables us to triumph over sin. Once forgiven, we enter God's heart, our original abode that once again becomes our safe harbor where our redeemed soul sails on in strength. Our end is not determined by where we began, but upon the choices you make and the directions we take. Our life is not limited by circumstances. The measure of faith we possess and utilize will determine our future.

God's Hidden Aspects

There are hidden aspects of God's being and facets of His nature that He has not revealed to anyone but Himself. God alone is God. God spoke His eternal words of wisdom and life into the sacred script of the Bible. His written Words give light to every person. God's Words are living, powerful expressions that quicken the dead back to life. God made His reality plain and clear for us to see through His invisible attributes. His eternal power and the mystery of His divine nature announce God's existence yet we do not bow in humble adoration to give Him the honor, worship and thanks He deserves. Instead we kneel in search of what we want and demand answers without offering a reverent heart.

God is always personal in His communication to all of mankind. The people championed in the Bible heard the majestic voice of God speak to them in their own language. When the invisible, Holy God revealed His face to people in the Bible, the result was always change. They sensed the awesome conviction of God. Gripped by terrible fear they fell down, in a powerless prostrate position as dead and were possessed by an overwhelming sense of their guilt and sinfulness. These people were forever transformed because they held an awesome fear and reverent respect for the terribleness of God.

Today most present a much smaller ignoble, weak God to the public because we do not see Him for the incomparably great God He truly is. Like the prophets of old our hearts should break with love until God's reputation is restored to the level of respect and honor He deserves. Let the voice of the prophets arise again to echo God's decrees; let the seers proclaim the wonders of what they have seen behind the veil, until every living person desires to know the immensity of the One True God.

When Moses saw the Lord in the burning bush he turned aside, removed his shoes and buried his face to the dust, afraid to look openly upon a holy God, lest he die.

When God spoke to Abram's empty heart he prostrated himself in the sand of the earth, paralyzed ready to pay any price. Abram intently listen to be filled with the voice of an Almighty God. We must submit to God with intent to obey His leading or there will be no meeting with God.

Isaiah, the prophet shook and trembled like the doorpost of the temple when he had a vision of God's holiness. He cried before a holy God of his own depravity, "Woe is me!" "I am undone, for I am a man of unclean lips."

Saul encountered the immense light and the voice of God on the Road to Damascus and collapsed to the ground helplessly blind. Paul regained his natural sight when He saw God in a spiritual visionary light and heard His voice speak within the confines of his narrow soul. How can mere men comprehend, much less explain, what they experienced, saw, felt or heard in the presence of a Holy God Who is beyond finding out?

To see the providence of God in our lives we must first enter into a calm quietness to daily listen for the heartbeat of God echoed in the stillness of His voice. In the tranquility of silence our heart learns to hear the inner voice, to know and reverence the presence of God who does not shout in the streets but whispers to the spirit. Many miss the manifestation of His presence because it comes like a gentle vapor resting upon the skin. Man looks for the sound of God's voice in the storms that rage, the lightening that splits the mountains and the earth that quakes and tremble at His presence. Yet God comes in the breath of His Spirit and looks to him who trembles at His Word.

Daniel stilled himself and saw a vision of Jesus on the twenty-fourth day of the first month of the year while he stood beside the Tigris River. Daniel looked up and saw a man standing in front of him. The man was wearing linen clothes. He wore a belt made of pure gold around his waist. His body was like a smooth, shiny stone. His face was bright like lightning. His eyes were like blue flames of fire. His arms and feet were shiny like polished brass. His voice was loud like a thundering crowd of many people. "I, Daniel, was the only one who saw the vision. The men with me didn't see the vision, but they were still terrified. They were so afraid that they ran away and hid. So I was left alone. I was watching this vision, and it made me fearful. I lost my strength. My face turned white like a dead person's face, and I was helpless. Then I heard the man in the vision talking. As I listened to His voice, I fell into a deep sleep, like a trance with my face buried in the ground. Then a hand lovingly touched me. When that happened, I struggled to get on my hands and knees. I was so afraid that my whole body was shaking." (Daniel 10:4–10 Author's paraphrase)

Whenever our holy God chooses to confront man's suffering and guilt by appearing to men, He maintains the integrity of His justice, mercy, grace and overwhelming compassion. The beauty of our Beloved infinitely surpasses all knowledge. The wisest intellects of man cannot tell us anything about the grace of God. God's grace and truth comes to us through Jesus who moves us into the depths of His boundless heart. The names of God are secret. His nature is unfathomable. God exists in Himself; His substance is unified and indivisible. He has revealed Himself to us by declaring the truths of His innumerable attributes. We humbly seek for God with a heart full of enraptured love. Love will open the gateways that lead to the heart of God. We ask in reverence, "Who is God?" and when we find God, we cry out, "How do we relate to Your perfection?"

God has no beginning or origin. He has always been and always will be. God is eternal; so He has no end. He is not affected by time, space or motion. God is hidden in an unreachable light which no man can approach. How can God who is exalted above the universe and our imaginations elude us, when all the while He is everywhere? If our imaginations were able to travel back to the pre-creation time we would find God waiting there for us with open arms. Without moving His eyes, with one all-knowing glance, God comprehends the whole of eternity including time past, present, and future in a unified instant.

Only by faith in Jesus and knowing His love are we able to glimpse a hint of God's beauty while He shelters us in the cleft of the rock and cradles us with His hand. If our faith is imperfect, our heart develops a numb insensibility to the presence of the all encompassing spiritual kingdom. A dull spirit does not allow us to feel the touch of the hand of God as He shields us from being overwhelmed by danger; so we cry out against Him, "Why are You allowing this to happen to me?" not realizing in reality He is protecting us. So, God silently waits in eternity for us to recognize the wings of His overshadowing presence.

Awaken Holiness

As sinful beings it is difficult for us to grasp the concept of true holiness when God is the only ultimate standard. We begin to formulate a religious list of does and don'ts to follow. If we follow them perfectly we are holy, if we don't, we are damned. Divine holiness is so far above us, we cannot understand how unapproachable and unattainable it is for natural man. Only the Holy Spirit can awaken holiness out of the measure of faith and illumine the truth we possess thus imparting the knowledge of true holiness in our humble hearts. God said, "Be holy for I AM Holy." No man is holy in himself. Holiness comes when we are covered by God's great grace which empowers us to act like Jesus in contemplation, speech and accomplishment. Here in the presence of a holy God we breathe pure, celestial air and listen to the poetic music of His existence.

When we truly seek harmony with God, we will journey into His heart, no longer hurting others in our thought life; or by speaking unkind, critical or judgmental words. When we are in synchronization with God we will no longer act in a harmful manner, we will have become holy. Renewed in the spirit of our minds, we go after peace with all men and holiness, without which no man shall see the Lord. The broken and contrite heart that loves God will not look down on people but has pity upon them.

Should we be like Moses who covered his face and clothed himself in humility and faith, so he could gaze at the face of God without dying? How do we take refuge in a God we cannot gaze upon but must hide in? How do we, like Moses, seek His glory yet hide ourselves in the cleft of the rock so God's hand can cover and protect us while healing our immoral condition, wounds and disease? God sees us perfectly through the precious blood of Jesus. The dreams God formulate help to disciple, enlighten our eyes to see Him and form us into suitable companions who will delight in the presence of a holy God for all eternity.

God is holy, high, lofty and exalted. He inhabits eternity and lives in the holy place. Clouds of darkness are around Him: righteousness and judgment are the habitation of His throne. God towers over all earthly things; yet He dwells in the hearts of His children so that He can live among people. His dream messages fascinate the hearer and revive the crushed spirit of the remorseful, humble hearted, lifting them upward. God's visions of divine transcendence give dreams of hope and life to the repentant soul. Repentance means to change one's mind, turn away from sin, and make a complete circle back to total dependence on God. Restoration comes to allow the fullness of the Spirit to dwell in us richly, in abundance and overflowing.

When the goodness of God shows Himself, our soul wisely cleaves to His greatness. The greatness of God stirs a reverent fear within us; but His goodness emits a peace beyond our understanding. Jesus said, "He that has seen Me, has seen the Father." We find grace in the eyes of the Father.

The Goodness of God

Oh God, my hope, my heavenly rest,
My all of happiness below,
Grant my importunate request,
To me, to me, Thy goodness show;
Thy beatific face display,
The brightness of eternal day.
Before my faith's enlightened eyes,
Make all Thy gracious goodness pass;
Thy goodness is the sight I prize:
O might I see Thy smiling face:
Thy nature in my soul proclaim,
Reveal Thy love, Thy glorious name.
Charles Wesley
6-8s. Exodus xxxiii. 18 – 23. A collection of Hymns 283

Dear Lord,

I pray through Holy Spirit because I know You will answer, and satisfy the hunger of Your treasured ones. I daily discipline and die to myself doing only what is right in Your sight. So it is by Your grace I am invisible, now hidden in Christ, so I can see Your face. In seeing You, I will be fully satisfied. Please draw near and bend down to listen as I pray. Show me Your unfailing love in wonderful ways. By Your mighty power You rescue those who seek refuge in You from their enemies. Keep Your eyes always upon me as You would safeguard the pupil of Your own eyes. Use the greatness of Your power to protect me from people who surround to attack me. Show me Your amazing loving, kindness and rescue me, for I depend on You alone. Hide me under the cool shadow of Your wings. When I rise up, let me gaze into the fullness of Your beautiful face. I long to see the grandeur of Your full stature. Let me hide in You totally absorbed in Your presence so I may live as heaven does on this earth. Amen

The Holy Spirit is always present; so He is always there with us in our dreams. When we are in His presence our heart is full of love for God. This overflowing love opens our eyes to see the majesty of Deity. The Holy Spirit graciously helps us search out mysteries and find the deep hidden treasures that are more precious than rubies, diamonds or fine gold. Men who's hearts break to know God are not understood by common man for they speak with a spiritual authority that comes from knowing God intimately. No man knows the things of God, for only the Spirit of God can reveal them to us as we dwell in the midst of life.

Our exact knowledge of God is but a shadowy form. When we are in His presence we give witness to the amazing things we see. We must continue to seek God's face to realize God's presence in His creation. God is faithful; He will never remove His lovingkindness. God is good, kind, benevolent, tenderhearted, and sympathetic. God dwells in an infinite environment; His generous Spirit surrounds and contains us through and through.

The knowledge that God is always present with us promotes an assured peace and blessed comfort. The world had its origin in the Word of His Spirit, thus God's Spirit sustains all things. He that comes to God must believe that He is. When we believe the Word of God, we dig out the unsearchable riches of God to experience the fullness of His joy.

Divine Treasures

True treasures do not lay on the surface to be carelessly swept up or gleaned. Seers and prophets express the greatness of God for their eyes have beheld His waves of glory; while scribes only dutifully write about the experiences of others. There is a vast difference between hearing the still small voice and seeing the matchless beauty of God. No longer competing with or desiring to please others, seers have given themselves totally to God. They remain focused upon the wonders of God's heart having penetrated the torn veil with intentional prayer and constant spiritual communion. The dream seer becomes what God has intended for all of us to be; totally conformed to the knowledge of the will and fellowship of God.

Our soul thirst to hear the sweet expressions of those who have drank from the living springs of water found in the depths of God. In those crystal clear living waters we live and move and have our being. Why do we remain without when the voice of the Bridegroom beckons to us, "Come, my shy and modest dove — leave your seclusion, in the secret place, in the cleft of the rock, come out in the open. Let me see your face, I want to behold your lovely form, let me hear your sweet voice. For your voice is soothing and your face is ravishing." The spring of morality is found in the deep love of Christ. What we as believers do as individuals, is what the church is doing as a collective body. God wants to impart Himself to the heart of our innermost being. How can we continue our spiritual progress, regain the use of His gifts and then sustain a high level in the glory? It is only by God's amazing grace that His Spirit reveals these realms to the Spirit of man.

Heavenly Mysteries

The mysteries that are in heaven are confined there until man reaches a spiritual maturity in the fullness of time to retrieve them. We are the ones who determine when we are willing to forge through the darkness to enter into God's splendid light of revelation. To see, hear and daily experience the unified threefold revelation of God requires a childlike trust, an extensive spiritual prayer life and meditation on the Word for physical preparation. The pure in heart will remove every veil of self-centeredness that separates them from the presence of God.

Those who submit their whole life to Christ shall see God's glory here on earth. God will reveal the things that dwell deep within that are separating us from Him. Layer by layer dream experiences uncover the sins that so easily plague us. When we yield to their messages, the sufferings we endure cause us to repent, thus removing another veil, bringing the loving face of Father God into focus.

God is always; previous, now and future. Our desire to pursue the person of God and to come and appear before the Spirit of God is created in God as He holds us securely in His hand. The thirst for the pure Word of God comes with an ardent love of the truth and an expectation to press in to hear the Father's heartbeat. To fully know an eternal God and His inherent personality cannot be achieved in a brief introduction or chance encounter but must be intentionally cultivated over a lifetime of intimately seeking His matchless face. This is eternal life, that we might know Jesus, the person of the one true God. When our spirit is quickened through a heavenly birth we begin the glorious pursuit of knowing the depths of the kingdom of God and are given the power to see the infinitely rich beauty that dwells in God.

"Blessed are those who are pure (Hebrew tohar, shining purity) and (darar, to become pure by separating oneself from all impurities) (Greek kathros, to be clean to have a clear, pure, guiltless heart and mind removed from everything that would distract your intentional focus from perceiving God)in heart for they shall see (Aramaic nizhon, dakay) God" (Matthew 5:8).

Jesus spoke the Aramaic word nihzon, which means to see and experience, through an abstract form, the essence of the richness of imaginative color and energy of emotions beyond normal perceptions. God is a supernatural invisible being because He is Spirit, love, the substance, power, glory and evidence of things hoped for in spirit and truth. We are made in the image of an eternal God so we also have the ability to experience and know Him. God can show us His glory and in a solemn procession of visions reveal aspects of His ways, nature and personality to us.

Can we gaze upon the transcendent beauty of our ethereal God? To see the wonders of God with the inner eyes of the heart is a Hebrew expression that indicates we can possess or acquire something tangible from God. The Greek word Opsoniti, from the root word horado, means to see by either a physical or mental image or an experience seen with spiritual eyes, a vision. To observe the beauty that rest in the realms beyond the natural, the real divine supernatural that very few see, one must intentionally look with a pure heart and continue looking until clarity of sight is given to behold the glorious colors and motions that exist past the veil.

Elijah told Elisha he must see him with purity of heart when he was taken up to heaven in order to receive the double portion of his spirit. Phillip's cry was, "That I might know God!" We must hunger and thirst after knowing God. If we are complacent we will not grow spiritually. When we desire God with all of our heart, He will be found of us. God waits to manifest His presence until our hunger draws Him into our realm. When the hunger of our heart touches God He becomes our inheritance; our true treasure, and magnificent portion wrapping all things up in one.

Transitions in Glory

We learn to transition from an earthly level of glory to an abounding expanse of heavenly glory when we seek God Himself and not His gifts, power or manifestations. For heaven to open its majestic heart, to release a transforming vision that reveals the knowledge of God and the power of God's glory people must acquaint themselves with the wisdom of God. The fear of the Lord is the beginning of true wisdom.

John the Revelator's soul cried out to see the majesty of God's face when he was ushered into the realms of the Spirit on the Lord's Day. John, the beloved, the personal friend of Jesus, was banished to the Isle of Patmos because of his passion for the Word of God and the testimony of Jesus, the spirit of prophecy. During John's years of isolation he learned to look into the invisible realms of the Spirit. The avenue to the depths of knowing God comes when we willingly walk through life's lonely valleys releasing our will and totally submitting to God. John was able to scribe the heavenly revelation of a future time. Instead of sinking into depression, his heart rejoiced over the mysteries of God.

John was liberated from a sense of needing material wealth, yet he possessed all things grand and glorious in the kingdom of heaven. John committed his all; his everything to the safety of God's loving hands. John gladly separated himself to focus on the Spirit of the Lord. God is the Spirit of Truth. Man can only know the greatness of God when he enters into the God's Spirit and Truth. John lived his whole life surrounded by the presence of God. His sacred isolation positioned him to receive the revelation of Jesus Christ. The great men and women of God are those who have totally given themselves to pursue God with all that is within them.

All of creation expectantly waits for the Holy Spirit's light of illumination to reveal the mysteries of Christ. Jesus is seated on the heavenly throne next to God His Father and on the throne of every believer's heart. John's spiritual eyes of faith were opened to see Jesus in His glory. Faith activates both our natural and spiritual senses to a spiritual kingdom that surrounds us about and within. The Spirit of God Himself showed John images of the distant future and heavenly visions. During his time of seclusion, John also saw a future door standing open in heaven. John's futuristic door is presently standing open to bring us into revelatory knowledge of the now! (Revelation 4:1) John's ears were tuned to hear the clarion voice of God calling him upwards to continue his higher pursuits of God. The voice of the Holy Spirit beckons each of us to recognize His absolute presence, to come up higher and transcend the limitations of our present reality. As gross darkness continues to cover the earth believers must enter into the heavenly realms of revelation knowledge in order to apprehend the wisdom that is needed to overcome the invading presence of evil.

At the time of his vision, John heard as it were the voice of Jesus behind him as a multitude of many flooding waters thundering. God has always trustingly allowed us to walk ahead of Him to make our own choices, to forge our own trail as He carefully directs our steps with the comfort of His voice coming from over our shoulders. His voice sounds like a trumpet resounding from the outer boundaries of the galaxy. John turned to see the face of the invisible One who was talking. He saw seven golden lampstands reflecting the seven rainbow colors of the Holy Spirit. (Isaiah 11:2) Then John saw the Son of Man dressed in a long robe, with a golden sash tied around His chest. His head and hair were snow-white like wool. His eyes were like blue flames of fire. His beautiful feet were like brass that glows hot in a furnace. Jesus held seven stars in His right hand. A sharp two-edged sword came out of His mouth. Jesus looked like the sun shining at its brightest time. When John saw Jesus he fell down at His feet like a dead man. Jesus placed His right hand on John and said, "Don't be afraid! I am the First and the Last. I am the One who lives. I was dead, but behold, I am alive forever and ever! I hold the keys of death and Hades. Now write the vision of what you see." The prophet John wrote with a spiritual authority and reported what he saw in the presence of majestic Deity.

The cultures of America (and many other countries) are cluttered with distractions which preoccupy our time and attention. If we take the example of John's banishment to the Isle of Patmos as prescriptive for our spiritual lives, we would need to make some changes to our attitude and actions concerning the proper use of time.

Instead of packing every waking moment with noise, activities and motion, we could emulate John by removing ourselves from our busy, frenzied lifestyle. A time of prayerful meditation and fasting without distractions, where we could actually feel the isolation and loneliness of life would go a long way to draw our attention to what really matters. The object of our life's, love and affection could turn from those temporal modalities, to the Eternal One, who is our all in all. We would stay close under the shadow of His wings declaring God is my help! My heart clings to Him and His right hand supports me.

Spiritual Enlightenment

Before sinful person can seek a holy God the Father must draw them through spiritual enlightenment from within. Otherwise, if we wait to pray while driving, the notion of visiting heaven while cruising down the highway at 60mph sounds a little stressful to the other occupants of our car. John pulled aside to look into the realm of the spirit. In the place of revelation his eyes were opened to see the door. Once John saw, he then heard a clarion invitation issued to come up to gain heaven's perspective. Revelation 4:1–2 After this I looked, and there before me was a door standing open in heaven. And the voice I had first heard speaking to me like a trumpet said, "Come up here, and I will show you what must take place after this." At once I was in the Spirit, and there before me was a throne in heaven with someone sitting on it" (NIV).

John the Revelator was issued an invitation to see future opportunities from a heavenly perspective. He entered the Spirit realm to access the door of hope by answering the call to "come up." God is not a respecter of persons. If He issued a call to John, then God has issued the same clarion call to you and me. Learning the ways of God will enable us to navigate the realms of the Spirit. Quiet times of prayerful meditation on and in the Word of God will enable us to interpret the impressions, dreams and visions God gives nightly to each of us. The love and peace of God has opened spiritual access and brings understanding to those who follow and respond to the call of Jesus. The world at large awaits the rise of clarion voices that have gazed behind the holy veil of Father's heart to boldly declare the tender mercies of the Lord that are new every morning.

"O my dove, that art in the clefts of the rock, in the secret places of the stairs, let me see thy countenance, let me hear thy voice; for sweet is thy voice, and thy countenance is comely" (Song of Solomon 2:14).

We must draw near to God to understand the secrets hidden within Him. Dreams are an essential to key to understanding who we are destined to become in Christ. Godly wisdom helps us address the negative interpretations that come from those who walk in spiritual darkness. It is critical that we give a free rein to the divine supernatural powers of heaven to rule in our lives. Every opaque veil of self that we remove brings us into more of the fullness of God's spiritual light revealing His brilliance.

Chapter 11
Ingenious Truth

Truth is conforming to a standard of integrity due to actual facts that lead to one's reality. There are various spheres of truth. Past truth, is chronological truth, our history that we forever memorialize. Present truth is the reality we are living in at the moment. Ingenious truth births fresh, new ideas and concepts we have not yet experienced or obtained yet. Ingenious truth leads to an innovative and creative future. To prosper we need an understanding of God's truth in each sphere. Past, present and future truths are equal in value, because one cannot exist without the other.

We cannot have a present or a future without a past. The dilemma with truth is we are comfortable with the known factors and parameters of the past. We recognize that our past history already exists; so it is easier to preserve and repeat. The future is full of unknown variables, so if we allow, fear can cause us to stay within a limited field of experience. Whereas, if we exercise faith, we will boldly step into the unknown with our confidence in God, knowing He has gone before us to prepare the way.

Our past has fashioned us into who we are at present. But the past cannot order who we will be in the future if we embrace our brilliant future with our hope firmly rooted in God. Habitually reflecting on past disappointment causes the memory to maintain a destructive connection with the past. The modus operandi of the enemy is to torment our minds as we imagine what could have or should have been. We are then filled with regret and shame rather than focusing on the possibilities that are ahead, and the wonderful promise God has made to fulfill our lives. The fulfillment of the promise He has made may often drag on for what seems like an eternity. As months turn into years, waiting can be crushing and even humiliating. We question ourselves; we question our reasoning; and the enemy will capitalize on our misery to the point where we may even begin to question God. Jesus inquired of His disciples, "Who do the people say that I am?" More importantly, Jesus made it personal when He asked "Who do you say that I am?" Jesus knew that when we place our hope in anything other than Him we will be disillusioned. Hope deferred makes the heart despondent.

It is imperative to always remember that God is exact truth and faithful. One of the names of God is Faithful and True. To move forward into our destiny we must completely disconnect from the disappointments, limitations, frustrations, and failures of the past. Ingenious truth releases creativity and enables us to press forward into our future with sharpened spiritual vision to confront all obstacles with imagination and resourcefulness. Ingenious truth will not manifest in the person who is continually looking back. Jesus warned of this when He said, "Remember Lot's wife."

Nothing exists in the natural realm until we are able to connect through observation. The words we speak paint a positive or a negative picture in the mind's eye. "The mind's eye can be defined as: the human ability for visual perception, imagination, visualization, and memory. In other words, the mind's eye is one's ability to see things with the intellect. Because many dreams are symbolic mysteries, God's guidance is necessary to uncover their hidden meanings. God intended that we get to know Him better through this process of discovering the meaning of our dreams. Our image center is a vehicle that the Holy Spirit can access if we are open to Him. The Holy Spirit will give us dreams in the night or streams of thought during the day to bring revelation and direction to our lives."[8] (Quote from Dream Encounters Seeing Your Destiny from God's Perspective by Barbie L. Breathitt chapter 2 page 24 Published by Barbie Breathitt Enterprises, LLC copyright 2009)

The way we describe an event causes the hearer to believe success or failure. Pictures are painted with thousands of words because they add the intricate details that frame the scenario. Visual memory is created through the hearing of the word. The spoken word through prophecy is a powerful tool that unleashes a person's potential when they mix the hearing of the word with faith. God's Word is progressive so it is always moving forward and active.

To apprehend the Word of God so that it lives largely and active within us will take a lifetime of making progress in our understanding of whom Christ is in us. God's goodness is great! The Lord has stored up and hidden many wonderful mysteries in His Word for those who fearfully follow and trusts in His ways, making Him their refuge. In the secret place of His presence He continues to hide us from the tongues of evil men who conspire against us. God shelters and protects us so His Word can have a starting place in us to bring forth an abundant harvest.

God's words have an ability to build, remove obstacles and clear a way to make new infrastructures. The holy God of eternity communicates with humble people who have crushed spirits. God's Word creates within us a new spirit full of hope giving us the heartiness to stand expectantly on our feet again. His Word heals our brokenness and places a new song in our heart. He leads us on firm paths and brings refreshing to our weary souls. New found comfort empowers us so we do not give up before we possess our promises.

Words are like seeds that are planted in the fertile soil of the believer. If they are protected, nurtured and watered with positive actions, they take root and spring forth with the ability to multiply their seed bearing potential. Increase, abundance and multiplication of life are in the power of the written and inspired spoken Word. When negative, critical or doubt-filled words are released and the hearer agrees, these words release death, poverty and destruction. When positive verbal seeds are planted in a soul, they grow the fruit of productive images in the imagination.

Negative word seeds grow visions of skeletons of lack staggering about in a shroud of scarcity and casualty. While positive seeds bring forth a healthy body gleaning a vast harvest of greatness, distinction, and prominence. Spoken words produce our future. When a constructive future is presented, agree with it. Liberate your inspired imagination to take it to a higher level. Observe the powerful picture as it is formed. When the vision is complete, allow it to imprint on your heart. Once it is imprinted on your heart, it becomes part of your spiritual DNA. This visual roadmap will lead you to destiny.

Why do we seem to obsess over hurtful things? Why do negative cycles of the past continue to manifest over and over in our lives? You have heard the expression "going around the mountain again." If we continue to make the same choices we always have, we will continue to obtain the exact same results. It is insanity to think that by habitually doing the same thing over and over we will receive a different outcome. A mental stronghold is a wrong pattern of thinking that leads to the formation of and an agreement with a harmful belief system.

When a harmful or limited belief system is established in our minds we will continually make the same poor choices. When we receive certain stimulus, data or input from people we automatically interpret their suggestions in a dark manner by processing it through the filters of our negative mental strongholds. They are saying one thing but we hear and understand them to be saying something completely different. Then in response to their input we push the same buttons and give them our automatic preprogrammed response.

In order to remove these negative, habitual patterns, the thoughts of our minds and the way we believe, must be changed, renewed and replaced with the promises found in the Scripture. What does the Bible, life's handbook, say about our situation? Ask God for His wisdom. In prayerfully applying God's good judgment, we will be given spiritual insight, to make the necessary changes that will break the destructive cycle of mistakes that causes us to "go around the same mountain" one more time. With a renewed mind we can then make the necessary shift to obtain a better future, on a higher spiritual level that is always spiraling upwards.

When we dwell upon the unpleasant things we have observed or experienced in the past, we give them the power to manifest in our lives now. We want to embrace a positive change and move on; yet the negative things we have endured try to hold us in a destructive thought pattern. As a person thinks, so is that person. Our mental focus will develop an image. Although the mind is multifaceted, if we focus on one thing, it is difficult to make room for or explore other positive options. We become fixated and limited. As we continue to meditate upon a mental image, our thoughts will eventually give expression through our actions.

Our daily actions and events form habits. Routine practices form a person's character. Moral fiber determines the level of blessing a person can sustain in his or her life. If a person has poor ethics and principles or lacks integrity, doctrine or true character, a ceiling is erected that prevents them from achieving their full God-given potential. A renewing of the mind must take place to build a stronger, broader foundation and new support structures must be erected for positive changes to spring forth (Deuteronomy 25:13–16).

We must stop dragging our past history of failures into our present, making our existence miserable. Repentance is a powerful force that will erase all our sin, pain, failures and regrets. The blood Jesus shed has the power to set us free from the past, propelling and thrusting us forward into a bright future.

Affliction has the power to bring needed transformation if we possess a teachable heart. Regrettably, the poor decisions we have made and the wrong actions we have taken produce negative fruit that can not be destroyed. We must take frequent personal audits by removing the pessimistic ANTs (A. automatic, N. negative, T. thoughts) from feasting on our picnics. The seeds we have sown will lead to results that are either good or bad. However, our omniscient God is a Great Redeemer, causing what was intended for our evil to eventually turn out for our good.

Yesterday's prayers, dreams, actions and decisions produce our tomorrows. Before a positive future can arise out of the grave of the past, we have to renounce our mistakes and stop rehearsing the harmful memories. Do not allow them to take center stage. Bury them and walk away once and for all, never to dig them up again. When the past wants to resurrect, change your focus to giving thanks for who God is, not just what He has done in your life. Celebrate the fact that God is the One and only God, Infinite, Eternal, Incomprehensible, Supreme, Sovereign, Transcendent, Majestic, All-Present, All-Knowing, All-Powerful, Forgiving, Loving and Unchanging Savior.

Dreams supply visions that give us a glimpse of God's image so we can begin to manifest His characteristics. The things we observe in dreams and the words we hear empower us to create a new scenario. Once something materializes in real time it cannot be undone; it is born into reality. Something that was once only maintained as a thought now exists.

When a dream comes, in order for it to manifest and be brought out of the spirit realm into reality, write it down. Faith takes action to bring about a work in progress. Then prayerfully consider the meaning of the dream. Dreams have different sources God, the soul, the spirit and the body and the realm of evil also tries to intrude at times. Ask the Holy Spirit to help you determine the source and the interpretation of the dream. We should never assume we know what each of the images represents. Always make a diligent inquiry of the Lord, seeking His wisdom and knowledge. Holy Spirit will give the needed skill and understanding as you continue to focus upon His beautiful, yet invisible face.

I am a certified dream life coach. If you are still not able to ascertain the meaning of your dreams I have created volumes of spiral bound, decoratively designed, laminated dream symbol cards that will give you both the positive and negative meanings of the symbols that appear in your dreams. You should also open an online dream journal at www.MYONAR.com and then submit your dreams to me for interpretation. Learning to understand the symbolic meanings of your dreams will enable you to succeed in new areas of your life.

Have you ever done or said something you regretted? No matter what you did or how many times you repented the results of your actions still prevailed. How can we undo something that is already done? Is it possible to redeem a negative situation and make it a positive one?

God created the heavens, the earth and all the living things that dwell therein. The nature of God is to create. He created both good and evil, darkness and light.

He fearfully and wonderfully created every person who has or will ever live. God created Jacob the scheming deceiver who always sought to place himself before others. Esau, his brother, tried to kill Jacob after Jacob deceived both Esau and their father in order the gain the blessings of the birthright of the firstborn son.

God had created Jacob with all of his short comings and weaknesses, but God did not leave Jacob in the miserable state in which He found him. God has the ability to create something out of nothing. God is also fully able to recreate something wonderful out of someone who will submit to His plan. Just like Jacob, God created each one of us, but He loves us too much to leave us in our former or present state of existence.

Because we are created in God's image, we are also creators. We are constantly changing, but are the changes for the better or for the worse? The decisions we make, the actions we take, the words we speak, and the dreams we have, all help mold us into the person we are destined to become. If we continue to maintain our present state of existence and never recreate any other alternative or opportunity for growth, we grow stagnant, meaning that rather than staying the same, we actually deteriorate and become stale. We find ourselves in a state of decline as the result of making no effort. Isaiah 43:1, Jacob, I the Lord created you. But I love you too much to leave you the way you are. I the Lord who formed you will now recreate you as Israel. God says, "Do not be afraid" the changes will cause you to walk into destiny."(Author's Paraphrase)

Two interesting Hebrew words: Created and Formed.

- Created[9]: OT: Strongs1254, HEBREW bara' (baw-raw'); means to create as a creator; to select or decide to cut down; to choose to continue to feed as a formative process: to make fat.

- Formed[10]: OT: Strongs 3335, HEBREW yatsar (yaw-tsar'); to form, fashion, frame, make or mold something earthen through squeezing it into shape especially as a potter molds the clay into a useful or beautiful vessel; figuratively, to determine to, place purpose into, (to form a resolution).

Once we have created something with our thoughts, dreams, words or actions, we must determine its purpose. Is it acceptable, good, excellent or bad? We must make a decision as to whether we want to continue feeding the thing we have created so it grows fat and prospers as it is or should we continue shaping, forming and remolding it to refashion it into something that has a greater or divine purpose? The things we create will either help us reach our destiny on time, delay its arrival or totally preempt it. What kind of a life have you created? God is the giver of life. What kind of life are you allowing God to create in you?

During life's journey we sometimes find ourselves winded, sleeping flat on our backs, staring up at the stars in a desert wilderness like Jacob. If we continue to dream and look up to see our redemption, we are sure to perceive our way of escape. However, if we stay riveted to our past history or present situation without releasing our faith to bring the future into our now, we will continue to dig a rut around the same mountain. To conquer these rocky territories in life we must explore various possibilities. Will we cast the mountainous problem into the sea, go around it, drill a tunnel through it, or overcome the mountain by walking over it step by step?

Caleb, the son of Hezron, and the father of Hur, was a mountain conquering champion. Caleb's name means capable, faithful one who is like a lion with great spiritual potential. He was sent by Moses to spy out the land of Canaan. He and Joshua were the only spies that brought back a favorable report. They were the only adults born in Egypt who entered Canaan as conquerors. He was one of the princes that divided the land. Caleb's life's philosophy was, "let us go up at oncc and take possession, for we are well able to overcome." At the ripe old age of eighty-five, Caleb remembered the Lord had promised him Kirjath-arba and the hill country where the strong, giant-like Anakim lived. Caleb drove out the giants, took possession and renamed the city Hebron. He did not allow his advanced age to prevent God's promise from manifesting. Nor did Caleb allow his current physical condition to enter into the equation. He claimed that he was as strong at eighty-five as he had been at forty years of age when he went to spy out the land that his natural physical strength had not abated. Caleb said, "If the Lord will be with me, I will take that land like the Lord promised me." He allowed the creative word of the Lord to strengthen and direct him to conquer his mountain. It was not Caleb's fault that Israel failed to go forward, but he suffered the consequences of the bad choices of others and was forced to endure the misery of delay. Caleb used his pretty daughter Acsah, a blessing that he "gained" while suffering the postponement of the promise, to his advantage, by promising her in marriage to the man who attacked and conquered Kiriath Sepher.

When we allow God to bring a greater measure of maturity to us as we wait on Him, instead of allowing bitterness or doubt to gain a foothold, the wisdom we gain will sharpen our spirits in future challenges that stand between us and our promise. When God blesses us, we have the power to bless others. Othniel defeated that city, so as promised Acsah married him. Othniel then told Acsah to ask her father Caleb for some more land. Acsah went to her father Caleb on her donkey. When she arrived, Caleb asked her, "What do you want?" Acsah replied, "Give me a blessing. You gave me dry desert land in the Negev. Now, please give me some land with water on it." So Caleb gave her what she wanted; he gave her the upper and lower pools of water in that land.

No matter how long we have to wait or which direction we choose to take, our hope must remain in Christ. He will draw us out of the natural realms of a desert existence and give us cool springs of water if we only ask. Holy Spirit places us on the ascending spiritual staircase of heaven. Although we are still going around now it is on a rising spiral staircase, so each time we take a step, reach up or make a lap, we find ourselves in a higher position.

Jacob saw the angels ascending and descending the heavenly ladder. God has called us to ascend that heavenly helix of revelation too. Jesus is at the top of the staircase, beckoning us in our upward spiritual journey. Step by step, rung by rung, we ascend into our spiritual destiny faith by faith; we go from strength to strength, always changing from one level of glory to the next. We are transfigured into the image of Christ as we draw closer to His all exposing light. The more we seek Christ the more we turn into the light of the Father. We become like the dense resurrection light that Christ radiated as He came out of the tomb. As we look on Jesus, we become like Him.

Chapter 12
Seeing Voices

Exodus 20:18, "And all the people were seeing the thunder (to yell, call aloud, a voice or sound) voices and the torches and the voice of the shofar (clear sound) and the mountain smoking; and when the people saw it, they trembled and stood at a distance."

Is it possible for people to see the multiple voices of thunder, lightning, and torches? Could Israel see the voice of the shofar while the presence of God caused smoke to cover the mountain? The term 'when the people saw it', ra'ah means OT: 7200 to see, to behold, to look on or upon, to discern, perceive, to experience, to meet what is present, to take heed, to respect the view or vision. They saw the lightnings and thunders which mean they saw voices. The Israelites were able to not only hear the loud peels of thunder crashing and the cracks of the lightning bolts they saw their voices with their eyes. This dimension of the display of God's glory must have been a terrifying sight. This visual demonstration caused their five natural senses to overload. There was a merging of the physical realm, into a spiritual conjunction that released a supernatural manifestation way beyond anything their natural senses could receive. They saw the physical manifestation of sound before their eyes. Their eyes heard and their ears saw both the physical and the invisible spiritual realms intertwined in a mystical display of God's power demonstrating His reality.

Everyone had come into a present unity where their spiritual senses merged to cause the commanded blessing to appear before their eyes. Their hearts were brought together as one people to learn to communicate in the realm of the Spirit before the One True Living God. This psychological neurological phenomenon is called "synesthesia." This dynamic interaction of a person's sensory pathways crossing, coming together or connecting in a unified, profound way happens to less than five percent of the world's population. Synesthesia which causes a heightened awareness, creative ability and compassion happens when one or more of the five involuntary senses of touch, smell, sight, sound or taste interact together with each other to perceive something all at once. The presence of God's glory hovering over the nation of Israel caused them to hear colors and the secret thoughts and intents of hearts, they smelled numbers, tasted sound, and saw voices. Could they have been experiencing what it was like to walk with God in the Garden before man's consciousness fell and was no longer able to tap into the higher spiritual sound waves of revelation knowledge? For a brief moment they were whole again. But, instead of rushing in to experience more of God their sinful state caused them to retreat in fear. How would you respond in a similar encounter? Have you prepared yourself for that magnitude of God encounter?

The prophets went to school to learn to understand how to commune with God with their hearts totally yielded to His will. The Bible tells us that God considers the prophets His friends; He remains close to those of a broken or contrite heart. Those like David who have learned to totally submit themselves to God's will and purposes. The prophets knew how to open their heart for God to remove the pain and disappointments by receiving His love. They were transformed into God's image through enduring the suffering of hardship for they knew it would work ability within their spirit to touch, hear, and see God in a new expanded way.

People fear the prophets who have joined their hearts to God; because they have an ability to see that which is normally hidden or unperceivable. The cloud of glory that descended upon the mountain opened all of Israel to the possibility of seeing and hearing the manifestation of God in a way they had never thought possible. But, even more than that, as heaven touched earth they were also able to see into the hidden recesses of their own heart and that of their neighbor's hearts as well to completely know the concealed thoughts of their mind. They heard everyone's secret thoughts as noisily as they heard their own. A man's lustful glance yelled out its intensions to a beautiful woman. A woman's jealous gaze loudly proclaimed how she really felt about her friend. Thoughts became like the voices of many waters merging together as a mighty crashing waterfall plummeting down the mountain. They were absolutely known by God, themselves and those they dwelt with, because the cloud of God's glorious presence had descended.

Moses had been through the process of opening his heart to God on a daily basis. His course had begun many years ago at his burning bush encounter. When Moses encountered the God of fire, he had responded much like the people of Israel. As Moses stood on holy ground, God drew him closer with His loving assurance that he would not die. The people of Israel chose to stand back and send Moses forward because they feared for their lives. They were not prepared to stand in the presence of such an awesome God. They feared this accelerated process of baptism into the burning cloud of glory would be their mortal end. Moses tried to comfort them as he had been comforted by God years previous but the people still stood off keeping their distance while Moses alone entered the fiery cloud of God's glorious presence.

We pray for the glory to come; for God to rend the heavens and come down, yet, do we really know what we are asking for? Have we allowed the fullers soap to cleanse us inside and out? Have we embraced the blood of the cross and its ability to purify the thoughts and intents of our hearts? What would happen if every one of our thoughts were made known and we knew the intimate thoughts of those around us? God is love. He operates in mercy, grace and compassion forgiving our sins and planning the best for our success. While we are judgmental, critical and unforgiving, holding ourselves and our neighbors in bondage to the same sins we ourselves have secretly committed. Is it any wonder why revivals or moves of God last for such a short time? Revivals come and go so quickly. Man in his weakened, sinful condition is not able to sustain a move of God's presence for any substantial length of time. When the anointing comes God's light reveals all of our blemishes, acts of flesh, and hidden sins. In the past, leaders instead of repenting, and adding their strength to the visitation, have become jealous, because the move of God did not come through them or their organization. They persecuted, condemned, and cast dispersion and derision on the ones who are operating in God's favor. It is the nature of man to criticize that which he does not understand. We fear what we cannot control.

The Bible tells us to call upon God while He may be found. "Seek the Lord while He may be found; call upon Him while He is near. Let the wicked forsake his way and the unrighteous man his thoughts; and let him return to the Lord, and He will have compassion on him, and to our God, for He will abundantly pardon. "For My thoughts are not your thoughts, nor are your ways My ways," declares the Lord. "For as the heavens are higher than the earth, so are My ways higher than your ways and My thoughts than your thoughts (Isaiah 55:6–9). God desires to sanctify our thoughts and the motives of our hearts so that we may become one with Him in the spirit of our minds. The pure in heart shall see God. When we see Him we will be like Him; able to dwell in His presence with clean hands to help touch and heal our fallen neighbors.

God has visited earth on many occasions. He walked and talked with Adam and Eve in the Garden. He appeared and spoke to Abram in dreams. God spoke with an audible voice and materialized to His prophets in clouds of glory on mountain tops. He appeared as light to Saul and as a burning bush to Moses. To Joshua, Jesus came as a Theophany, or the Lord of Host. Jesus, the Son of God, came as a baby, lived among men demonstrating the love of His Father. Christ died on a cruel cross, was buried and resurrected to ascend back to heaven. The Holy Spirit visited mankind on the Day of Pentecost through the sound of a mighty rushing wind and tongues of fire that rested on the heads of the hundred and twenty. That historical event was a foretaste of the powerful visitation God has scheduled for us today. Throughout history we have celebrated the Day of Pentecost with the hope that God would send the fire with a new sound to rest upon His people once again. When believers awaken to the great potential that God has placed within us, as the sons of God, the whole earth will respond to the manifestations of God's Word spoken through faith filled individuals. When a spiritual unity is released through the power of love and we arise as one people nothing will be impossible. When each person yields their strength, anointing, and faith, a corporate body of Christ will arise as a glory cloud with healing in their wings. The greater works generation will come forth covering the world with unprecedented signs, wonders and miracles. The resurrection of the dead will be common place; no disease will be able to stand in the presence of this mighty God resting upon His purified bride.

A Vision of Mass Miracles

About twenty years ago, the Spirit of the Lord came upon me as a golden shaft of heavenly light. Every earthly thing that surrounded me seemed to disappear as I was totally consumed by the presence of celestial beings. The Holy Spirit and several angels appeared above my head in a beam of light. Suddenly I found myself being translated to heaven in this cylinder or light field. The angels surrounded me as we ascended up to heaven in the most beautiful passageway of white living light. The powerful light was so brilliant my body vibrated with the force of its energy. My flesh felt like it was supercharged with electricity. There was so much light present that my body became transparent. I was given an awareness and internal view of every cell of my being. Each minute cell rejoiced in the light of perfect love knowing it had its own identity and purpose. Although there were countless millions of single cells they were all divinely connected, to act as one unique body, to accomplish destiny. They were stimulated to reach their peak performance, resonating with eternal life, and tuned to receive the harmonious sounds of wisdom.

Heaven's perfection and beauty was beyond anything human words could describe. I saw and experienced the vast grandeur of heaven's endless dimensions but that was not the purpose of my visit. God wanted to share the future with me. The Holy Spirit and the angels wanted me to see the plans they had reserved for various large stadiums around the world. During those moments in heaven I experienced the greatest outpourings of the Holy Spirit which rivaled anything I have ever read about in historical accounts, seen, or heard foretold.

The heavenly host took me to stadiums jammed with overflowing crowds of people. Every stadium seat was taken; it was filled beyond capacity. People were standing in every available space. The ground floor was packed like a sardine can with wall to wall bodies. The grassy fields were plastered with sick people, the terminally ill, the dead, and the dying were brought in by families in hopes of experiencing a miracle. The hospitals had lined the playing field with the stretchers of people suffering from assorted incurable diseases and physical maladies. The parking lots were blocked with ambulances, campers, cars, vans, and buses. The masses of people were all intently focused on receiving a touch from God as they pushed their way in against the heaving press of humanity. They forced their entrance into the stadium. Only one thing mattered; they had to encounter the living God.

The enormous stage was equipped with bright flood lights. A booming speaker system broadcast the unknown voice of a person above the noise of the desperate crowd. The person on the microphone was an intimate friend of God; yet unknown to man. They were familiar with God's ways, His healing and miracles and the moving of the Holy Spirit. The person on the microphone was given different words of knowledge by the Holy Spirit. This would signal the crowd when to release their faith, step into, or reach up and touch the electrified cloud of God's presence. The thick presence of God's power swept over the masses to release healing for Aids, cancer, leukemia and other terminal diseases. The voice would echo God's directions, "Step into the flow of the anointing, release your faith, and receive your healing." A massive golden cloud of glory rested over the top of the stadium. The roar of the cloud could be heard, seen and felt for miles. Within its mystical borders exploded lightening, gold dust and the intertwining flight of thousands of miracle healing angels. God's glory cloud would descend from the top of the stadium to engulf the sea of humanity as Holy Spirit swept over the expectant crowd. God's magnificent presence would descend from the top of one side of the stadium bleachers until He permeated the people on the ground floor. When the mass of infirmed people were touched, healed and delivered the glory cloud would ascend to the top of the opposite side of the stadium and come to rest again.

As the illuminated, mist of the amber, glory-filled cloud engulfed the people; they were instantly healed by God's vibrating power. The masses of people who were already healed were crying, dancing, singing, laughing and rejoicing in the goodness of their God. Soon men and women ushered them out of the stadium. This made room for those who were still pressing their way into the stadium. When the cloud came to rest at the top of the stadium the voice would announce which disease or affliction the next move of the Spirit of God was going to heal. Then God's glory cloud would once again engulf the people in His tangible warmth and weighty miracle presence. The cloud of the Lord's phenomenal power would settle on hundreds and thousands of people in one swift sweep. The Holy Spirit's healing glory and goodness passed over each individual person simultaneously just like a giant light filled scanner or Xerox machine.

No one praised the anointing or gifting of a famous man or woman. Only God received the accolades of the people as they were healed. The person's voice on the microphone was only necessary to tell the people which healing anointing was present. That way the crowd could release their faith to receive their healing or miracle as God's presence and goodness passed over them.

In front of the stage, ordinary, everyday people like you and me were rushing from person to person laying hands on them and seeing astounding miracles take place. Missing limbs were growing back, empty eye sockets were being filled, and every conceivable body part imaginable were being restored in front of their very eyes. The dead were being raised to life again by children, teenagers, housewives, business men and women. In this faith filled atmosphere of anointing an electric energy of faith was released by all the expectant people coming into unity. God released the commanded blessing! The people knew that in the presence of an all powerful God nothing was impossible! With God nothing is impossible!

Chapter 13
Communicating with Nature

Elijah the prophet was able to shut up the heavens to prevent rain for three years. Elijah had a father's spirit which trained Elisha so that he would exceed him in ministry to be able to carry two times the anointing of his spirit. Elisha knew how to communicate with nature. He instructed the mother bears to judge only forty-two of the boys in the crowd of youth who mocked the ways of God by rending them in pieces. "Then he (Elisha) went up from there to Bethel; and as he was going up by the way, young lads came out from the city and mocked him and said to him, "Go up, you baldhead; go up, you baldhead!" When he looked behind him and saw them, he cursed them in the name of the Lord. Then two female bears came out of the woods and tore up forty-two lads of their number. He went from there to Mount Carmel, and from there he returned to Samaria" (2 Kings 2:23–25).

Have you ever asked yourself why Elisha sent the two bears against forty-two youth and not the whole lot? Forty-two is the number connected to the anti-christ, it represents religious flesh, man's opposition to God and His will, trials and Israel's oppression. When forty-two of the youth died, it sent a message that God is Lord and His purposes will prevail. The number two means separation, division, contrast, split, war, testimony, witness giving support to judgment, ruin and death. The anti-christ spirit was removed allowing for the positive aspects of the number two, God's revelation of blessings, multiplication, and harmony in the living Word to manifest. Revelation knowledge comes through intimate times in the presence of the Lord.

Daniel's heart knew the discipline of communing in prayer with God and angels.

He learned the secret of how to converse with lions when he was unjustly thrown into their den. He became aware that the pride of lions was apparently on a “Daniel Fast!”

Jonah was able to communicate with nature. Jonah refused to take his call to deliver his enemies in Nineveh instead he fled the presence of the Lord and boarded a ship destined to Tarshish. A terrible storm arose. The men on the boat cast lots to determine why the destructive storm had come. The lot fell to Jonah. So he encouraged the men of the ship to throw him overboard. Jonah found himself treading water in the sea. The Lord sent a great fish to swallow Jonah. Jonah prayed to the Lord from the stomach of the whale shark for three days and three nights. The whale shark followed the Lord’s command. He carried Jonah to God’s desired destination and then spit him out on dry land. (Jonah 1:17; Jonah 2:1–10) The word of the Lord came to Jonah a second time. This time Jonah accepted his prophetic assignment. He had three long days to think about his message as he walked to Nineveh.

Then Jonah walked for one more day through the city he cried out and said, “In forty days Nineveh will be overthrown.” The people of Nineveh believed in God; and they called a fast and put on sackcloth from the greatest to the least of them. When the word reached the king of Nineveh, he arose from his throne, laid aside his robe from him, covered himself with sackcloth and sat on the ashes. He issued a proclamation and it said, “In Nineveh by the decree of the king and his nobles: Do not let man, beast, herd, or flocks taste a thing. Do not let them eat or drink water.” “But both man and beast must be covered with sackcloth; and let men call on God earnestly that each may turn from his wicked way and from the violence which is in his hands.” “Who knows, God may turn and relent and withdraw His burning anger so that we will not perish.” When God saw their deeds that they turned from their wicked way, then God relented concerning the calamity which He had declared He would bring upon them. And He did not do it (Jonah 3:4–10). God had mercy on 122,000 people and their animals.

Balaam didn’t understand the body language of his donkey when she ran off the road, then smashed his foot into the wall and finally lay down under him, but Balaam clearly understood the words his donkey spoke to him. “Balaam was angry and struck the donkey with his stick. And the Lord opened the mouth of the donkey, and she said to Balaam, “What have I done to you, that you have struck me these three times?” Then Balaam said to the donkey, “Because you have made a mockery of me! If there had been a sword in my hand, I would have killed you by now.” The donkey said to Balaam, “Am I not your donkey on which you have ridden all your life to this day? Have I ever been accustomed to do so to you?” And he said, “No.” Then the Lord opened the eyes of Balaam, and he saw the angel of the Lord standing in the way with his drawn sword in his hand; and he bowed all the way to the ground (Numbers 22:23–35).

During the great flood Noah and his family lived with every animal and creature that was known to earth. When the flood began to subside Noah spoke to the dove three different times as he communicated his assignment before he sent the dove out (Genesis 8:8–12).

When the two hundred and seventy-six men that were aboard the ship that wrecked with Paul swam to dry ground, the village people of Malta welcomed them with extraordinary kindness and a fire to warm themselves by. When Paul had gathered a bundle of sticks and laid them on the fire, a viper came out because of the heat and fastened itself on his hand. When the natives saw the creature hanging from his hand, they began saying to one another, "Undoubtedly this man is a murderer, and though he has been saved from the sea, justice has not allowed him to live." However Paul shook the creature off into the fire and suffered no harm. Paul carried a powerful anointing. He understood the blood of Jesus was the anti-venom to the viper's poisonous bite and the source of healing for every sickness and disease. Publius, the leading man on the island, hosted and entertained the crew for three days. After that Paul went to the home of Publius's father who was lying in bed afflicted with fever and dysentery. Paul prayed, laid hands on him and healed him. Then the rest of the people on the island who had diseases came to Paul to be cured. Paul knew how to communicate with a snake to overcome and nullify its dangerous poison. He also knew the words to destroy the effects of invisible microorganisms that caused sickness and disease (Acts 28). Prayer in the name of Jesus is an all powerful force.

The hearts of these men were one with God. The Bible states that David was a man after God's own heart. God desires that same heart condition for all of us. The Bible makes it very clear that the pure in heart shall see the multiple unlimited dimensions of God.

Jesus as our example was able to communicate to His Father in heaven, the Cherubim, Seraphim and the angelic realms, people, to Satan, the demonic realm and to animals. Jesus and the disciples landed in the country of the Gadarenes (Matthew 8:28–34). There they were met by two demon possessed men, coming out of their home in the cemetery. These men had intimidated that area for a long time until no one considered it safe to walk near that region anymore. When the madmen saw Jesus they screamed out, "You're the Son of God!" Isn't it interesting that the demonic realm had no difficulty identifying the anointing on Jesus while some believers and churches still struggle with it? The demons screeched out of the men, "What business do you have with us? Have you come to punish us before our time? You weren't supposed to show up here yet!" The evil spirits begged Jesus, "If you cast us out of these men's bodies, let us live in the herd of pigs rooting in the distance." Jesus granted the demons access to the herd of swine. Once the animals were possessed by the evil spirits, they became crazed with fear and the whole herd stampeded off the cliff and drowned in the sea. When the pig herders reported what had happened to the towns people that the two possessed men were delivered and sane but the herd of pigs had been destroyed the people rose up in fury. They were angered at the economic loss the death of the pigs represented. They feared the power Jesus possessed so they demanded Jesus to leave their province.

We worship and adore the God who fearfully formed us in our mother's womb. Daily He watches over our developmental process. He sees us in and out of our darkest hour by immersing us in His divine light. God knows how we think and feel in the darkest trials of the night so He instills hope for our tomorrows. When our hope is placed in God and God alone, we have the power to change. There is nothing in heaven or on earth that can hide us from God's watchful gaze. The darkness of night is not darkness to God. It is as bright as the noon day sun. God knows our now, our future and our past, nothing escapes His tender watchful gaze.

As I shared earlier in my Mallard duck encounter God often speaks to us personally through nature. Everyone's home is their sanctuary. But, we want God's presence to dwell in our homes, in our bodies and personal surroundings at all times. Years ago, I asked the Holy Spirit to indwell me, to always surround me especially when I traveled. I asked my friend Holy Spirit to watch over me, in my home, in hotels and on airplanes. He has always been faithful to watch over and protect me in every situation and to manifest wherever I have gone.

Early one morning before the sun had risen; I awoke to the sweet sound of turtle doves cooing at my bedroom window. I knew it was the manifestation of the Holy Spirit wooing me. I snuggled in my warm bed as I intently listened to the loving words He spoke so tenderly to my heart. When I opened my front door to take my miniature Pomeranian, Super Duper Mini Cooper, for a walk, to my surprise, I found that a beautiful pair of turtle doves had built their nest in the rain gutter on my porch.

The dove is the symbol of love and of the Holy Spirit that came to rest upon Jesus, the precious Son of God. Doves are interesting animals in that they have a single focus; they only look at one thing at a time. When the Holy Spirit is gazing upon you, you are His total focus. The dove is a symbol of a gentle or innocent person, an advocate of peace, a heavenly messenger who brings harmony and deliverance.

In the (Song of Solomon 6:9), King Solomon refers to his lover as a unique, perfect, pure, blessed dove. Then King Solomon, as a symbol of the Holy Spirit, woos her "O my dove, in the clefts of the rock, in the secret place of the steep pathway, let me see your form, let me hear your voice; for your voice is sweet, and your form is lovely" (Song of Solomon 2:14). He longs to be with her, "I was asleep but my heart was awake. A voice! My beloved was knocking: 'Open to me, my sister, my darling, my dove, my perfect one! For my head is drenched with dew, My locks with the damp of the night'" (Song of Solomon 5:2). When I would read and pray in my back yard the doves would come to roost on the top of my fence. When traveling they would come to roost in the windowsills of the host homes or hotel rooms. Doves began to show up everywhere I went. I knew the Holy Spirit was surrounding me with His peace that passes all understanding.

Once I was a guest at a famous evangelist's home. I asked the Holy Spirit to give me a sign of a dove that He had divinely orchestrated this connection. Within a minute a beautiful turtle dove landed a few feet from where I was sitting on the sun deck. Then as a second sign, I asked God to send a male dove to join the female dove so it would not be alone. Within a few seconds another dove landed on his back patio. These two doves acted as if they were tame pets walking within a few feet of us. As if that was not enough of a confirmation, I asked the Holy Spirit to send a jeweled hummingbird. Hummingbirds represent 'fruitfulness that comes from cross pollination of two streams or plantings of the Lord. The sweet treasures of life will bring a rapid success from a small beginning that will become as tasty as a busy bee's honey formed from the flower's nectar.' No sooner had I finished praying within my heart than a beautiful jeweled throated hummingbird came buzzing onto the scene. God has sent two turtle doves and a hummingbird to confirm a Holy Spirit relationship. God is so good.

Hummingbirds have shone up at healing conferences too! Steven, my brother, saw a hummingbird try to fly into one of our meetings in Houston. The little fellow hit the windowpane and fell into the bushes. Steven rushed out to rescue the stunned bird. He gently cupped him in his hands and carried him to the front of the church. The presence of the anointing quickly revived the little hummer. Then, Steven carried him out of the building, opened his hand and watched the little hummingbird fly away. The Lord spoke to me, "It is not about the mega numbers it is about empowering the small people exercising their gifts at the kingdom gates of cities and nations. Small is the new big!"

Chapter 14
Time and Eternity

Dream communication comes from a variety of sources: from the body, from the depths of our soul's yearning, from the evil influences of mischievous spite, or from angelic messengers and, of course, from the imaginative heart of a loving God. The Holy Spirit lingers over, surrounds, and daily indwells mankind. He embraces us during the night season, and gifts us with His dreams or what I call God's visual love letters.

The Holy Spirit is the master change agent. He hovered over earth's creation when it was dark, formless and void. The Holy Spirit's captivating power, light and magnetic eternal life-force established the boundaries of land and sea as He followed the creative directives of God's commands. The Holy Spirit creates something tangible out of nonexistent material. God is the only being who has the ability to take nothing and make something stunning. God makes everything beautiful in its proper time and season. He has placed eternity in our hearts; yet we are still not able to comprehend the magnitude of God's mighty works.

The Living Word divided darkness from light; cast chaos away; established order; beauty and symmetry. The Holy Spirit's presence indwelling us has the same effect on our lives. He enlightens us with wisdom, answers the longings of our soul, gives clear insight, divine direction, and releases a peace beyond our natural understanding. When our soul remembers God's benefits, He pardons all of our iniquities, heals our diseases, and redeems our life from the pit of destruction, crowning us with lovingkindness and the tender mercies of His great compassion. God satisfies our lives with good things. When we understand that God has given redeemed man's dominion over everything, including time, we are able to recapture the years the locust have destroyed and renew the years of our youth, like that of King Hezekiah.

The dreams that God chooses to arouse within us beckons us to chase after knowing Him throughout all of eternity, with all our heart. Before time began, while we were still in the heart of God; the dreams that would call us into destiny were sown in us. Once we were born, the path God designed for us began to arise out of our innermost being. Our spirit hears and responds to the call of God. The small inner voice and internal vision God placed within us, causes us to connect with our heavenly Creator. Worshipping God in the eternal realm of the Spirit empowers the Holy Spirit to direct us into our destiny, purpose, and call. Trust in the Lord with all your heart, and lean not on your own understanding; in all your ways acknowledge Him, and He shall direct your paths (Proverbs 3:5–6).

The eternal mysteries God locked within our spirit create urgency within us to seek after Him. God alone holds the key that unlocks the time capsule of revelation He deposited within us. Dreams enable us to receive revelation knowledge and vision, so we can then operate outside of time, to release the miracle realm. Those who trust God, will never be forsaken, or found begging for bread. When we seek God with all of our heart, we find Jesus, the only door of access; when we connect to Jesus, He is found of us. The Holy Spirit connects our soul to the living God, the heavenly Jerusalem, and to an innumerable myriad of angels. These angels celebrate the community of firstborn, who worship God, the judge of all. These realities can be grasped by the soul when an eternal heaven collides with people dwelling on earth in a dream, vision, or a time free spiritual zone.

God created time for man to learn how to operate in and out of the confines of the natural. We were created in the realms of eternity; we are eternal beings who have been placed in time for a brief moment. God placed eternity within our spirit and then strategically positioned each one of us in a specific time period to release our measure of eternity into the history of now. Time is a substance and a tool for man to use for our benefit. If we sow time into the kingdom of God we can also reap time to spare.

God's love for the world was demonstrated in that He gave His only begotten Son, Jesus, so that whoever believes on Jesus, their life shall not pass away, but they are given an eternal, perpetual life without interruption. To be absent from this mortal body is to be present with an immortal, incorruptible God. When we are born again, that which was mortal is swallowed up by life eternal. God's incorruptible spirit enters our spirit and we become immortal. Eternal life is that we may know the one true God and His Son, Jesus Christ who was sent by the Father.

Eternity is the perpetual, continuous, and uninterrupted, inexhaustible discovery of more knowledge of God's unending attributes while being surrounded by His love and glory. Eternity is more than the unending bridge that reaches beyond the expanses of time's beginning and end. Eternity is best pictured as a circle which has no beginning and there is no end point. Eternity is an arranged combination of past, present and future all wrapped up in a progressive proceeding now. The more knowledge of God and His ways that we possess the more our mind is renewed and transformed into the mind of Christ. Knowledge of God enables us to destroy speculations and every lofty thing that rises up against the understanding of God. By taking every thought captive to the obedience of Christ we are able to release the kingdom of heaven on earth.

In the beginning Adam had favor with and dominion over time. If Adam had not fallen to sin; he would have never aged or died. Jesus' death and resurrection restored divine healing, prosperity and everything including time to man when Jesus entered back into the realms of glory.

God has given mankind dominion over every created thing. Psalm 103:5, reminds us to bless the Lord at all times and not to forget all His benefits. God forgives all our sins and iniquities, heals all our diseases, redeems us, and satisfies our years with good things so our youth is renewed. King Hezekiah is a great example of God turning back time for fifteen years to bring healing and restoration of youth.

The visions and sacred dreams we dream that are inspired by God, give us temporary entrance into the portals, windows, doors and gates that open into heaven. These spiritual gateways and their network of openings are known and guarded by a myriad of angels. When these doors are open, during certain seasons and times, or through sacrificial giving, prayer, praise and worship, we are able to glean revelatory knowledge and an abundance of blessings if we have humbly positioned our hearts to receive through repentance.

The Garden gate where God walked and talked with Adam was a portal. Once man sinned, an angel was released and stationed at the doorway of the portal so man could no longer access the realms of the spirit where he had previously walked with God before the fall. The exact location of the Garden's gate though sought, has never been found, because it was a spiritual portal. Enoch walked with God through the portals of eternity rising higher and higher. He was engrossed in maintaining a perpetual quest for more of God. Enoch explored the rich depths of the fresh manifestations of God's infinite being. Enoch passed through each new chamber and heavenly doorway until he was no more. He did not want to return to the lower levels of spiritual existence once he had tasted of heavenly bliss. For Enoch to be drawn back into this lower realm of survival, where the measure of revelatory light is so dim, would have been unbearable after he had been enveloped in God's glorious realms of enlightenment.

There are appointed times in the Spirit (Leviticus 23) and seasons of holy convocations that when carefully followed open portals of blessings upon the seeker of God. The children of Israel were allotted a window of opportunity, a certain amount of time to pack their belongings and exit Egypt. The Lord opened a portal of escape (Exodus 3:8) that allowed the Israelites' to pass through the Red Sea on dry ground. After the appointed time was over, the Red Sea closed itself up again, drowning the whole Egyptian army before they could flee Gods' judgment. There are many examples in the Bible of God opening spiritual portals, gates, windows and doors for His children to discover, explore, escape through or encounter Him in.

Malachi 3 tells us that the Lord we seek will suddenly come to His temple. We are the temple that the Holy Spirit comes to visit. But if we have not been purified by the refiner's fire, smelted as silver, refined like gold and washed with fullers' soap how will we be able to stand to give the Lord offerings in righteousness? The Holy Spirit draws near to judge each of us nightly in our dreams. If we have strayed, like the sons of Jacob, in a backslidden state; Holy Spirit urges us to repent and return to Him, with all of our hearts. When we rob God in any area of our lives especially in tithes and offerings we are cursed with a curse, so no matter how hard we try, nothing we do, will work or prosper. But if we fear the Lord, give reverence to His name and bring our whole self and the entire tithe to those who feed us spiritual food, God promises to open the revelatory windows of heavens' provision and pour out a blessing for us that will overflow our boundaries. It will be more than we can personally contain, so we will have enough to help all nations. God will also rebuke the things that devour our understanding, like the religious traditions of man. We will find God's blessing resting on everything our hand touches; our time, health, relationships and promotions will all exceed our wildest imaginations.

We are able to redeem time. Let me give you an example. There was a conference in Dallas with a wide selection of speakers and ministers. Some knew how to follow the leading of the Holy Spirits manifestations and others did not, they just shared their own message. All the leaders were seated on the front row awaiting our time to release what Holy Spirit had shown us for the people present. During the worship segment, a miracle anointing was released from heaven for signs and wonders to take place. However the person leading the meeting at that time did not discern the shift in the atmosphere. My heart was grieved as the anointing came, lingered and then began to lift since it was not engaged or utilized. Holy Spirit is a gentleman and will not force His presence on anyone but waits for us to surrender to His plans and purposes. I knew by a word of knowledge that there were ten people present that desperately needed a miracle to heal their terminal heart conditions. I sought the Lord. What do I do? Do I just sit here and let this opportunity pass knowing people need Your touch? Or do I interpret the leader and ask if I can minister Your healing presence? The Holy Spirit told me to "Sit tight." He said, "When it is your time to minister you will redeem the time when you felt the miracle anointing come. Simply release your faith to go back in time, enter into the miracle portal then claim and release the anointing for the ten who need their hearts healed." I was excited to know that God is God even over time because He is eternal and operates outside of our programs and time schedules. Revelation knowledge releases power to change natural elements by releasing miracles.

Dreams and visions allow us to exit this temporary realm where we are confined by time to enter into the eternal creative realm where there are no limitations of any kind. As we learn to understand how our dreams relate to the sovereign times, dates and seasons set by God, we will be better able to align ourselves with Gods' perfect timing to obtain spiritual understanding and insights as well as His miracles, signs and wonders. When we are dealing with Gods' times on the earth, it does not depend upon the amount of faith we posses. It has more to do with our ability to understand His eras and respond properly in the correct seasons, like the sons of Issachar. When the portal is opening, we must move quickly in obedience, we must enter in while there is availability. Once the aperture of the gate or spiritual doorway closes, it is possible that we will not have another opportunity to enter into the fullness of blessings, until another season in time. The way that we respond to the Holy Spirit's leading and our dreams, at set times of the year, will determine the rest of that year, specific cycles and can affect us for many years to come.

The supernatural gifts and revelation knowledge we receive in our dreams and waking times prepare us for the events that are to follow this season of shaking that has come upon the earth. Those who love God with all their hearts have been reserved for the Kingdom of God, the best of times; these last days, because they have an uncanny hunger to pursue the powerful presence of God.

We have entered a time on earth that has never taken place before. Higher levels of angels are opening heavenly manuscripts, books and scrolls for us to read, declare and sing. The words of wisdom these volumes contain are hand written upon the tablets of our hearts. These higher hosts of beings are now visiting people. The thoughts that are being inscribed in the dreamer during these visitations will ignite a new belief system that will inspire them to move in power through these higher realms and ways of God. The revelation that is assigned to us in visitations enables the dreamer to become the messenger who is assigned to reveal that supernatural realm of understanding to others.

Our dreams help us fill in the basic elements of faith so we can bring forth the supernatural manifestations of God. The more we know God and understand how to operate with angels in the dream realms of glory the easier it will be for us to step into the supernatural realms to retrieve miracles during our waking lives. God sends His angels to protect us, to render service or run errands for those who inherit salvation and speak the Word of God with faith.

My brother Steven is my ministry administrator. He often travels with me when his work load allows but, he had to stay back on a recent trip to Colorado. The host mistakenly put me at a motel where the room doors opened to a noisy parking lot. That night, as I tried to sleep a rowdy motorcycle gang of drunken, unruly men and biker babes pulled up. They were loud and proud, shouting obscenities while they kept circling the parking lot looking for trouble. I knew the only thing standing between me and that disruptive band was a thin motel door. When Steven travels with me I always feel protected and looked after but, he was in Texas this time. So I prayed asking the Lord to send His angels to protect me. When I opened my eyes again Steven was standing at my hotel door. Well, it wasn't really Steven; it was his guardian angel that looked exactly like Steven. The angel smiled real big at me. Then, he stepped in front of my motel door, folded his arms and took on a formidable stance. All of my fears and concerns for my safety lifted and a supernatural peace settled in enabling me to sleep. My short prayer had gone out in a matter of seconds to draw in the host of heaven.

Our spiritual DNA outlines and communicates God's plans and purposes through a microscopic sensory web. Obedience to His Word brings revelation knowledge which cause accurate perceptions of visual images in our lives and dreams to take shape. God can project images of our sin, physical weaknesses, disease and error in our dreams to warn us of their destructive nature. We are then given the choice to repent and replace them with His forgiveness, powerful presence, anointing and revelation that gives us the ability to overcome. Each individual chooses whether to receive revelation knowledge and then apply it to their life.

There are many forces that can influence our destiny or spiritual DNA. We determine which force will control our destiny; God's love—, self, darkness, or the lust of the world. Each person must distinguish God's spiritual DNA in their life, to activate their destiny for godly purposes rather than for evil or self-fulfilling purposes. A new God-consciousness arises out of a repentant heart enabling us to taste and see that the Lord is good. Jesus, the true light of life, brings real enlightenment to every man coming into the world. (John 1:9) God's presence whether in the dream realm or in our waking lives becomes the glory and the lifter of our head.

O God,

I pray that You quicken into existence and multiply the power that flows from every ounce of faith that is within me, that I may grasp eternal things. Open my blinded eyes that I may see Your glory now in the land of the living; enhance my spiritual perception and acuity; enable me to taste Your goodness and see your mercy. Make heaven more of a reality to me than the earth I dwell on now. Amen.

Chapter 15
Thoughts Produce the Person

Positive creative thoughts make a person superior; while negative, destructive thoughts breaks the person. The expectations we possess and the thoughts we think within the mind have the power to mold, reorient and make us better or worse. Our thoughts are the creative tools that shape and bring forth lives full of joy or sadness. The things we ponder in our heart and think about in the quiet recesses of our minds are eventually birthed into a reality.

The environment we inhabit is shaped from our secret thoughts and our response to the way we interpret the dreams we dream. Our minds develop, store and build upon the thoughts we think. Our thoughts eventually become the memories we continually visit. In time we will see our quiet thought processes amplified, magnified and colorfully imaged in the reflections of our ethereal dreams.

Dreams reveal the perceptions of the things we believe to be truth. The virtue of the thoughts we encourage lays the foundation of our belief system. Dreams weave the inner fabric of our character. The colorful entwined threads contained in our dream murals show us where we have strengths that flow or where we are knotted up with weaknesses. Our character is the summation of all of our thoughts and the meditations of our hearts, thus it produces our actions. Every thought continues to grow until it manifest through an accomplishment or detrimental action. The decisions we make and the actions we take produces the world in which we live.

Godly character produces a holy environment; while negative thoughts produce despondency, depression, poor character and polluted surroundings. God encourages us to think higher thoughts. The Holy Spirit inspires right thinking because it will bring about an abundant prosperous life. Higher thoughts lead to superior ways; as a man thinks in his heart so is he.

Spoken words are a reflection of the depths of the waters that run through our lives. The naïve individual speaks of trivial matters, they are a narrow sway because they are always tiptoeing in the shallow waters near the safe shore line. The spiritual person possesses a rich wisdom and a wide depth of influence. The ripple affect of spiritual wisdom inspires others to mirror the words she speaks and the actions she promotes.

God causes the flowers to blossom at certain specified times during the day. The great botanist, Linnaeus, once said that if he had a conservatory that contained the right kind of soil, moisture and temperature, he could tell the time of day or night by the flowers that were open and those that were closed! The thoughts we deposit within our heart bring forth seeds that produce a plant after the likeness of that seeds DNA. The plants continue to mature until they bud and blossom producing flowers. Each flower's bloom proudly announces the birth of a new thought. The flower produces the fruit that contains the seed. Have you ever noticed that the word seed has the word 'see' within? Every seed that is within us will bring forth a specific type of harvest that others will see and enjoy or despise. When the kernel germinates it showcases the silent thoughts which are finally seen. Both the intentional and the impulsive seed thoughts we sow and then cultivate will bring forth the next generation of fruitful harvest. What kind of harvest are you reaping? Good or godly thoughts will bring forth a blessed harvest of humility and servanthood which is true greatness in the eyes of Jesus. Negative, critical, doubtful or cynical thoughts will develop a negative harvest of lack, despair and poverty. God sends us dreams that help us take inventory of our lives and accurately view our present level of spiritual, emotional and natural developments.

God originally placed Adam and Eve in The Garden to tend, cultivate and take dominion of the earth. There He daily walked in harmony with them in the cool of the evening. After they sinned; the sound of the Lord's voice lovingly calling for their company stuck terror in their hearts. They hid themselves from His presence. We have been called to tend and cultivate this same secret ground, the sacred garden that lies within each of our lives. Here in the secret place of the soul, God calls out to meet with us daily. Will we make time to listen, to walk with Him and talk with Him in the holy place of our temple? If we spare no room in our garden for God, nothing of value can grow. What we take time to plant will grow. If the weeds of loneliness and compromise invade our lives and they are not removed quickly they will multiply and take over. To compensate for our aloneness we begin to fill our lives with social engagements, entertainment, worldly pleasures and pursuits until God the Master Gardener is expelled from our private garden shrine.

God is the standard by which we must align every thought, action and deed. Without Gods' loving presence to correct and prune us we become unfruitful entangled with the weeds and ensnared by briers. When we allow the things of the world, even companionship, to crowd God out of our garden, He is not able to cut away the dry barren branches so we cannot produce spiritual fruit that brings forth eternal change. We are the garden of God; so we must hear the voice of His presence every day.

The actions and reactions we manifest in our dreams are the sweet or embittered fruit of our veiled thoughts. People continue to grow or they diminish according to the philosophical concept of the causality of the law of cause and effect. These laws state that an action or event will produce a certain chain reaction or response which manifests in the form of another event. These laws are hidden in the invisible realm of thought before they manifest their fruit in the natural. Sowing and reaping is a universal law that no one can escape. We often sow in tears before we reap joy in our lives. The verbal or material seed thoughts we plant will spring up and reproduce after their kind.

Righteous character is not a chance happening. It is sculpted from many years of devoted concentration on the right, noble, pure, godly thoughts and focuses. But if one chooses not to embrace higher thoughts and ways, they will continue to wallow in the miry pits of desperate need, decay and desolation. The way we perceive things will cause our thoughts to either be born of our own self desires or we will hold our thoughts to the obedience of Christ. If we settle for meditating upon or acting on, our lowly thoughts, they will never cause the higher affect and life God desired for us to manifest. God desires us to view things from a heavenly perspective. I would encourage you to purchase my book "DREAM ENCOUNTERS: Seeing Your Destiny from God's Perspective" to gain further insights from heavenly perspectives.

Make a once and for all time commitment of your entire being to God. Do not hold anything back; give your all to Jesus. The things that we hold back and try to manage ourselves are the very things that cause us suffering. Letting go and keeping an open hand before the Lord insures He can easily remove harmful things from us and replace them with good gifts. Serve and obey God's direction through the written Word and the Holy Spirit's guidance. Godly commitment causes our eyes to see the faithfulness and righteousness of God demonstrated in our lives. Choose to walk in godly obedience and do the works of righteousness in thought and action.

Righteousness positions us in right standing with God and man. When we have favor with God and man we prosper and increase in every direction. Jesus learned obedience through the things He suffered. We learn obedience in the same way. Jesus was obedient to His Father's will even unto His death on the cross. We are to take up our crosses daily. The benefits of righteousness come by obeying the written Word which grows the fruit of right standing with God. An intimate loving relationship with Jesus allows us to adapt His divine nature, sanctify our thoughts and imagination and surrender the will of our soul, to the rule of the spirit.

Sanctification and obedience to God's leading brings our thoughts, function and deeds to a new level of commitment to God's will. When every member of our body is totally committed to God's ways, the Holy Spirit will lead us in a higher more noble way. We will discover all truth is revealed to those who live holy lives that are set apart and dedicated to God. When we love God with all of our heart and our neighbors as ourselves we will not do anything harmful or wrong towards anyone in either thought or deed (Romans 13:10). When we reach this level of maturity in love, the greater works Jesus spoke of us doing are finally released. Our sanctified imaginations or renewed minds are to be used to see the glory realms, discern the Father's will and bring heaven to earth.

Every Believer can hear the voice of God and be led by the Holy Spirit because God's sheep hear the voice of the Good Shepherd and follow after Him. Good servants follow the Master's voice in complete obedience to what He commands. Godly obedience leads to righteousness. Righteousness or right standing leads to sanctification which is the beginning of learning how to live a holy life. Holiness is the gateway to unconditional love towards our enemies and all of mankind. Holiness leads to the demonstration of the greater works. And Jesus replied, "You must love the Lord your God with all your heart and with all your soul and with all your strength and with your entire mind; and your neighbor as yourself" (Luke 10:27).

This Scriptural mandate is a true challenge. Those who allow God to take them through the pruning, breaking, reorienting and the fiery refining process are molded into golden vessels which are utilized by the Master's hand. However, few are able to surrender their dreams and life's aspirations yielding their whole being, body, soul and spirit to this level of conformity to the narrow, straight ways of God's will because the road less traveled can be both arduous and lonely.

God makes it clear He is the only One who can direct us onto a higher path when Jesus said, "For My thoughts are not your thoughts, neither are your ways My ways, says the Lord" (Isaiah 55:8). The decision to ascend onto the Highway of Holiness (Isaiah 35) means we are trusting in God's righteousness in every area of our life. We have surrendered all, to walk a committed live of total dedication to God. The belt of truth sets us free when we keep it centered on our waist. The truth of God's Word directs our steps, guards our hearts and minds and keeps us stayed on Christ Jesus. When our thoughts, will, and actions are totally committed and focused on Jesus and the purposes of God's kingdom we will faithfully display His breastplate of integrity and morality.

The decisions we make whether noble or ignoble are followed by consequences. By making God the Lord and Master of our life His Word will renew the thoughts of our minds and the intents of our hearts. God is one hundred percent committed to us. So we should be secure in totally committing ourselves to Him. We can trust that the things we commit to God are kept protected. "For this reason I also suffer these things; nevertheless I am not ashamed, for I know whom I have believed and am persuaded that He is able to keep what I have committed to Him until that Day" (2Timothy 1:12). God is worthy of total trust and our highest praise.

Have you heard the term a self-made man? As we apply the principles of thoughts birthing actions and actions birthing habits, while habits birth character, which determines a destiny, one can clearly see that the thoughts we harbor will determine the lives we live.

A person's subconscious and conscious thoughts form the person; be they great or small, rich or poor, saved or unsaved, noble or ignoble, wise or ignorant. Dreams are a useful component to bring forth and reveal the things that are brewing below the surface in one's subconscious being. Dreams reveal both our weakest beliefs and our strongest views.

The thoughts we think become the building stones of life. What are the materials you are building your life with; precious gemstones, gold and silver or wood, hay or stubble? Some of these materials will not stand the test of time. When the fiery trials of life come, if we have not built on Kingdom principles, everything we have built will be destroyed and only the ashes will remain, until the winds blow them away leaving us with nothing but sorrow and regret. We need to build on a strong biblical foundation with gold, silver and costly jewels that have been tried and tested in the fires and pressures of life.

I awoke one morning to an audible voice whispering, "Wood, hay and stubble!" My first response was fear; knowing Holy Spirit meant the fire of God was coming to test my life's works. But, I also knew that in the mercies of God I needed Him to judge what I had built; if it was not pleasing to Him, I still had time to make the necessary changes. I wanted a crown to lay at Jesus' feet when I entered

His presence. Whatever I had fabricated that was not of Him, or built on His pure principles would not be able to stand the fiery furnace. False motives, selfish desires, pride and ego seeking would all be destroyed, reduced to ashes. But, that which was of Him, the tried and true, the pure, the holy, the precious and undefiled would become as pure gold and glistening gems in the Master's hands. God is so good that He promises to give us beauty for our ashes when our works are burned up; if we will trust His judgments to be true.

The contemplative planning that goes into our vocation forms the life we live. Fire tests everyone's work, while exposing the under lying motivations. The results of our labors become glaringly plain for all to see in the bright day light. If we build on a firm, godly foundation our life will stand the fiery tests of time. In the end we will gather a reward as a faithful, wise servant. But, if the life's temple we are building burns, crumbles, or falls apart during the shaking, we will suffer great loss.

Our mental activity develops and strengthens our character; it brings joy or sorrow, success or failure. Jesus said, "If a man sees a woman and lusts after her in the thoughts of his heart, he has already committed adultery with her." This is an example of one of God's higher ways. He considered thoughts to be on the same level as the actual sin. It is a fearful thing to imagine all of our thoughts being posted for others to view and then being held accountable for them.

The thoughts we think and the deeds we sow also form the level of rewards, stature and magnitude of the mansions we will possess in heaven. With that in mind it is important to consider what spiritual tools and divine materials are we using to framc and build eternal life? The Word of God has the power to change and transform us. It will renew the mind, wash away sin and grant us wisdom beyond measure. Praise and thanksgiving draws God's presence and multiplying power into every situation. The right thought life combined with wisdom and proper choices will insure a promising life here and in the here after.

A person will either skillfully create a prosperous now, a bright future or continue to break themselves in the dismal recesses of their mind's thoughts. People determine the level of divine perfection and fruitfulness their soul will ascend to or the depths of abuse they will allow their character to descend into by the thoughts they entertain.

Each of us is given keys that lock the doors of harmful, negative influences or unlock any and every door of opportunity. The keys we choose to use in life determine which doors we possess walk through and which doors we shut or remain locked. We have been given the keys to access a heavenly kingdom and bring it into existence here on earth. If we use the right keys God's kingdom authority will manifest from within us and fill the whole earth with His goodness and greatness.

If we carefully follow the purposeful plan that God has crafted for each one of us, the keys we possess will continue to unlock the doors that attempt to block our forward momentum. Prosperity requires us to keep our eyes focused upon the prize. By daily seeking God with a new determination we continue to move forward with the insights Holy Spirit shares. Pray as if your today and all your tomorrows totally depend upon God and work as if your success depends utterly on you. To receive an answer to prayer requires that we exercise a feat of trust or faith exploit on our part.

Liberty comes as new doors are explored with confidence and the different fruits they offer are collected, tasted and shared with others. It is always more blessed to give than to receive. Blessings will multiply when one continues to give and pass the blessings they have received onto another. But, those who selfishly hold back good from others, who are in need, when it is in their power to bless, help and increase them, will end up in poverty.

A new harvest grows when we skillfully steward the seeds we have been given or collected by planting, tending, watering, weeding and harvesting in the fullness of time. A few positive seed thoughts will reap an abundant harvest of new opportunities. No one saves the seeds that come from a poor tasting fruit or a vegetable of no quality. But many collect the seeds that come from a delicious garden so they can reproduce the best crop possible the following year. It is the same with our seed thoughts. Collect and save the positive thoughts as cherished memories; but cast down the vain imaginations and trample them underfoot using them as a stepping stone to reach a higher elevation.

Meditating on godly thoughts aids our mental, physical, and spiritual development. Thoughts shape and can then reshape the conditions that exist in our life. Creative thoughts can transform the images of things we see in the Spirit. When ingenious thoughts materialize they will empower us to change our status in the natural. Our thought life determines whether we will rise above circumstances to benefit from them or fall victim to them being crushed under the weight of trying to carry them on our own.

Dreams show us our current condition. Dreams are also a barometer that governs the changes that need to happen in our attitudes or actions. Do your dreams show you as well mannered? Do you have a gentle loving, nature or are you caustic and explosive? Does anger erupt when you are under pressure? Dreams reveal invading weakness or blind spots that once recognized, can be repented of and then transformed into strengths once their root cause is discovered and their lie is exposed, discredited and removed. To properly analyze the coded message a dream delivers, a reflective, diligent search for truth must take place. When the dreams' code is broken, it will empower us to become master life builders and destiny designers.

We are then able to consciously remove faulty foundations and questionable coverings to use both our intelligence and constructive energies to rebuild on God's established truths. Any negative thing such as unforgiveness, isolation, bitterness, shame, guilt, depression or hatred that we have hidden in the closets or basements of our lives can now be detached from, swept out and removed. By eliminating past emotional hurts we make room for a brand new chapter in our lives to begin. Why hold onto the old festering wounds when trusting in Jesus will make us whole again?

Truth will always set a person free to produce eternal fruit, even if there is pain involved in the discovery. Jesus knowingly carried all of our pain to the cross, so we do not have to bear it, release it to Jesus once and for all.

When we prayerfully examine our self we will discover the dark secrets that lurk within, by exposing them to God's light, we can uproot them and cast them aside. Once the wrong root thoughts are removed their poisonous fruit will dry up and their cancer will disappear, never to return. Please avail yourself to the beautifully designed Healing Card I have developed that will help you determine the root causes of major sicknesses and disease. When you pray against the root causes the unholy fruits of disease dies and dries up releasing your healing. www.BarbieBreathitt.com

Once we begin to accurately discern our thoughts and the cause and the effect they produce in us, as well as in those around us, we are able to observe, manage, frame and adjust our negative or nonproductive thoughts to improve our lives and fulfill our destinies.

While we are mining our soul for understanding we will also discover beautiful jewels shining from within, the unique formations of precious stones and the valuable many faceted diamonds that have been fashioned and cut through the intense pressures of life. The fiery trials of life will produce a pot of pure, transparent gold once the dross has been skimmed off the top. We will look like the pure translucent gold that paves the golden streets in heaven.

Diligent, godly reflection enables every distraction and sin to be revealed so it can be removed. God utilizes every life experience whether good or bad nothing is wasted. Holy Spirit is able to cause every difficulty and disappointment in life to work together for our benefit in obtaining a working knowledge of His ways and an understanding of ourselves. The patient seeker of God's invisible face is left with a wisdom, knowledge and clarity of self that reflects the purity and power of the Maker of our soul.

To cultivate the soil of one's mind, in order for it to bring forth a fruitful harvest, the negative weeds, impure, wrong and wild briery thoughts, must first be pulled up, cast down and consumed in the fire of the Holy Spirit's love. Once the ground has been cleared of non-productive or harmful, thorny foliage, new-productive, life-giving seeds must be planted in their place. As a master gardener one must realize that it takes time for a seed to geminate, take root and sprout to bring forth a new harvest. Be gentle, patient and long suffering with yourself and others. Practicing patience and diligence is necessary to cultivate a fruitful mind of positive, productive, pure godly thoughts.

As a man thinks about himself, so is he, becomes true because our thoughts eventually form actions which structures our character. We discover who we truly are when we find ourselves crowded into a corner or crushed under the unjust circumstances of life. The pressure we endure from without open us up to expose the tender areas that rest within. Just as a beautiful rose when pressed releases its fragrance so when the forces of life come to devastate; the real person who lives within is freed to manifest either their bestial, brutish nature or the sweet fragrant aroma as their inner state of being arises.

The circumstances of life allow us to make choices. The choices we make and the actions we take demonstrate our character. The internal person steps out from behind the mask and makes itself known. We will either display the beauty or the beast that lies within. Every person displays the inner workings of their personality when outer forces are at hand. These forces reach into the deep recesses of our mind, to unlock the closet doors where the skeletal thoughts we so carefully hide reside. Once the door is opened our thoughts step forward as they are given a voice that boldly makes their presence known.

Our actions demonstrate our pleasure if we have found harmony with God's divine nature. Our actions will also announce and display our discontentment to a harsh unjust environment. No matter where we find ourselves in harmony or in disarray the thoughts we think enable us to progress, learn and grow spiritually or they will cripple our forward momentum and trap us in the quicksand of regret. As long as we succumb to outside forces instead of allowing change to come from within, where the Holy Spirit dwells, we will continue to fall victim to or be limited by circumstances.

We are not to be controlled by outside influences although they are often used to redirect us onto the proper path. God has given each of us the power to create and recreate through pensive prayer and declarative speech. As we flow in God's creative rhythm things begin to change and line up with His plans.

Wisdom breaks up the fallow ground of our soul so we do not waste our time or energy sowing among the thorny thoughts of past failures. Gather up all your regrets and cast them into the fire. It is important to prepare the heart for God's plow to drop into the rich soil of the soul. His presence will enrich our lives by digging a deep fresh furrow where new seeds of thought can be planted. Our individual lives change to the degree that our mental disciplines exhibit self-control and our lives are altered depending upon the clarity of our prayer.

Rapid changes take place when we assume responsibility for our thoughts and actions submitting to the Holy Spirit's skillful molding of our character and working in our lives. Until our minds are renewed and changes are made, our wounded soul will continue to draw the same type of people who create adverse situations in our lives. The soul is a magnetic force that attracts like souls into its company. Like begets like, and birds of a feather flock together.

To experience growth one must have opposite or opposing forces within their lives to affect an iron sharpening iron occurrence. The objects and people we cherish, as well as the things we dread, are all hidden within the chambers of our heart. We wrongly think no one will know our secret thoughts if we don't give verbal expression to them. We reveal who we are when we talk because out of the abundance of the heart, the mouth speaks. Thoughts eventually produce actions, whether they are viewed in our dreams or solidified in our waking lives. Even when our thoughts are not shared with others verbally often they are still heard by those who are spiritually perceptive. Actions produce habits and habit produce a destiny. The longer we keep our negative thoughts greedily hidden within, the longer they will continue to draw those same forces, toxic people and destructive elements into our lives.

What's In My Heart?

Quiet my soul,
Who will know
This King without the decadence of silence?
Sorting through thoughts,
Which one is You?
Which one is not?
Brooding in my heart,
Knowing in part (1 Cor. 13:9),
Wanting to be whole.

Who will know
This Healer apart from His Words?
Into my heart transferred
Alive off the page (Heb. 4:12),
Dining with a Sage,
The profound is heard
And now preferred.
What was blurred
Now shines bright like a diamond!
What once clutched tight
Dimming my sight,
Has been laid low at His feet
On His footstool......
Where earthly judgment
And enemies bow (Isa. 66:1; Luke 20:43).
This key to how
My heart stays clean
Swept of bitter and mean,
Gems and prizes now seen.
What does your Spirit say?
Hidden manna for today (Rev. 2:17).
Incline my heart to your testimonies (Ps. 119:36),
With evil I will not agree,
For as one thinks in his heart,
So is he (Prov. 23:7).
So fail me not, heart!
LIGHT penetrate
Every vessel, atrium and chamber,
Atmosphere changer,
I believe my new name (Rev. 2:17)!
Into Your rest, I will labor,
For who can know
Lest he listen and order his thoughts
With the pulse of the King
Empowering to fight this Philistine (1 Sam. 17:32)!

By Shawn L. Martin

People often comment that they do not know why they continue to draw the wrong type of people into their lives over and over again. But it becomes obvious, upon conversing with them; the negative issues of their hearts make it abundantly clear. Their words release a clarion call that draws people who embrace their harmful philosophies of life. They have not repented, renewed their minds by washing away negative thought patterns or established new ones that are written in the wisdom of the Word of God. These individuals are blind to the negative mental-strongholds they have erected and to the fortress of pessimistic emotions that dwells within. As long as they continue in these same negative thought patterns they will continue to make the same mistakes in their personal, business and social relationships.

Every pessimistic word or thought that is sown and not plucked up will eventually take root and bring forth a harvest after its own kind. Briar seeds bring forth briars. It is insanity to plant orange tree seeds and expect a crop of corn to spring up. Godly thoughts produce godly actions and responses; while evil, dark-thoughts bring forth sin, sickness, lack, disease, destruction and major chains of limitations. The world that surrounds us, both the enjoyable and the unfriendly, comes from both our positive prayers and our negative reasoning abilities, mental powers and the aspiring thoughts and desires we ponder within.

We must realize there are people in our lives who need our help. These people did not come to ruin, or to their end-of-the-line experience, over night. It was a long arduous path filled with wrong intent and bad decisions, followed by negativity, pessimism, and doubt. Unless a downward mental cycle is broken and then reversed, one will continue to be dominated by wrong thoughts that find them stranded on a dead-end road. A person's mental processes and their character actions manifest as one. A person's character outwardly demonstrates the inner workings of the heart. The circumstances that surround us are the outworking of vital developmental elements that abide within our essential mental processes. Our thoughts determine how much we can achieve. They also project the level of success our character can maintain.

Life does not happen by chance or probability but by the law of sowing and reaping. Input equals output. If we sow a wrong thought we will reap a negative outcome, disrupting a harmonious flow resulting in discontentment and disappointment. If this harmful cycle is not broken, repented of and a new healthy thought pattern sown, the outcome is disease. The circumstances of life are a wonderful teacher. We learn, grow and expand evolving into a healthy fruitful being with every spiritual lesson we master.

Every trial once successfully completed enables us to add new knowledge to our storehouse of mental wisdom producing spiritual and natural wealth which graduates us to a higher realm of thought. God said, "My thoughts are higher than your thoughts!" Everything we experience in life both the excellent and the awful are redeemed by God to bring us into an elevated place of existence in Him.

The circumstances in life prepare us to ascend up the spiral staircase of mental, emotional and spiritual development. Life is full of suffering. Jesus was acquainted with grief and He learned obedience by the things He suffered. As we learn to embrace the sufferings that come from time to time, we will be able to breakthrough the realm of soul and enter into the realm of manifesting the Spirit of God's glory in our lives.

When we walk by the Spirit we receive revelation knowledge which quickly matures us, so the mind of Christ, which we possess within, can be revealed outwardly for all to see. True spiritual maturity allows us to count it all joy when our faith is tempted and our trust is tested in trials and tribulations that come at us from every direction. When we are under extreme pressure our faith life is forced open. The pressures of life cause our inner workings to be revealed, showing our true colors. We learn to develop patience and perseverance during times of suffering. Never try to short cut the process God has designed to perfect the things that concern you. If we preserver through the challenges of life they will do a complete work in us and the end results will be good. We will not be deficient in any way, we be well developed, lacking nothing, mature in all that God wants us to be.

Man is defeated by circumstances as long as he wrongly thinks of himself as a being that is formed by outside conditions that produce suffering or hardship. Remember, fate does not dictate poverty or restrict our outcome, but one's undisciplined groveling leads to morally wrong thoughts and abasement. Stop asking, "Why me?" Instead, ask, "What am I to learn from this test? What harmful way is God trying to remove from my thought patterns so I can be promoted and rise to the next level of excellence?"

The buffeting of life's circumstances does not form a person but it reveals their character to them. We are able to command that the seed hidden in the soil of our minds will produce positive life bearing fruit. Freedom comes when we realize that God has given us the ability to rule over ourselves, by mastering our thoughts, and words, which then produce actions full of creative power. Every thought we have becomes either a positive or a negative producing seed when it is planted in the fertile soil of our minds. When a seed falls to the ground it dies and brings forth a multiplication of fruit after its own kind. God is the Master Gardener and fruit inspector. Will the fruit your life is producing please Him?

Negative thoughts produce the fruits of suffering in negative circumstances; whereas positive life-giving fruit seeds blossom into positive actions which produce the peaceable fruit in abundance. The outer manifestation of the world that surrounds us and the things we reap comes from the harvest of both the pleasant and unpleasant inner thoughts of our hearts.

When we adopt and follow godly principles of self-control and purification we create a wonderful life. We are able to change the conditions of our circumstances to the degree we alter our mental capacity to think on godly things. Once we receive the mind of Christ we can then decree and command life to line up with God's nature and plans. God's plans are always for us to prosper and succeed as our soul (the mind, will and emotions) prosper.

When one discerns a flawed character or defect, repents and prays for wisdom, supernatural guidance and asks God's assistance in changing both their thoughts and actions, great grace is released. The implementation of prayer brings forth a suddenly; allowing quick changes to take place in our developmental processes. Prayer changes things in the mental and physical realms of our existence.

Repentance will cause the negative things we once attracted to us through our wrong thoughts and faulty belief systems to change. We will begin to attract positive productive elements and people. The soul has the power to attract the things it loves and hates, dispelling or repelling fears and aspirations according to the secret desires and thoughts it hides. The soul will rise and fall in accordance to its highest ambitious pronunciation and will be dominated by its lowest un-chastened desires. The dreams we dream help us to keep our finger on the pulse of life. Are we racing off on the path of destruction? Or are we walking hand in hand in harmony with the God who lovingly created us to succeed?

People who have a noble character have spent many disciplined years developing their intimate relationship with God to gain His wisdom and higher levels of correct thought. Honorable behavior does not come by random opportunity or because a person is favored more than others. Integrity is developed over time. Character is built line upon line and productive thoughts are erected upon constructive reflection and positive actions. Good deeds lead to a kind, tender servant's heart that is full of love and compassion. The Fruit of the Spirit becomes the tools by which we build a strong character, form joy and peace in our earthly lives and construct the vast scope of our heavenly mansions too.

People who have lowly thoughts also have ignoble character. Do not trust them. The words they speak are not true. They are full of tricks and conniving scams, always seeking ways to cut corners to take advantage of the goodness of others for their own benefit. They are eventually captured by the weapons and snares they formed to destroy others. The evil man's arsenal and destructive armory is eventually turned towards himself. The traps he so carefully laid for others will ensnare him in the end. He will be destroyed by his own wayward devices. One lie leads to another, until his life story is so distorted and confused that he can not remember what is true or false. Thus calling evil good and good evil, he falls into a pit of self-destruction.

A person does not come to the tyranny of destruction unless their thoughts continue to dwell on an evil path. God is merciful. God sets up many roadblocks and detours to deliver the soul who seeks His guidance and instruction. No one is suddenly plunged into debauchery. It is a slow and steady dedication to the descending thought processes of depravity that leads them to their destruction.

We do not attract the things we want, but that which we are; "dogs beget dogs." Our passing impulses, desires, and life ambitions are opposed and frustrated at every turn. Our inner intentions and dreams are developed and continue to grow with the foods of polluted poison or the pristine thoughts that we feed them. Our base thoughts capture and then enslave us to a life of habitual disappointments. Our destructive actions restrain or imprison us with chains that bind and manacle our ankles, limiting our field of influence, progress and success, which eventually renders a just sentence of failure. No one can run a race to win if their ankles are shackled by the iron weights of sin's limitations.

The prayers of the malevolent go unanswered for his heart remains black and cluttered with evil schemes and deceit. He prays for relief from his suffering yet continues to seek his own self-gratification. He does not want to repent, change or improve his animalistic nature. His own desperate thoughts and primitive actions continue to confine him to his own stony hearted prison.

The sinner strikes out and fights against his outward circumstances but continues to nurture his inward, conscious perversion and the depravity of his heart. His own unconscious weakness and moral frailties retard his momentum. He will remain in this defeated state until he calls out for God's intervention and help, repents of his vices, asks for mercy, and renews His mind with God's Word.

Mankind wants to live in a paradise of utopia where they dwell in the ease of abundance and grace, but they refuse to go through the process of developing their character to strengthen their moral existence, so they can possess and contain the blessings they desire.

To gain more, one must develop their spiritual understanding and wisdom so they can sustain greater realms of influence and responsibility. If one does not sow the time and effort that is required to improve both their relationship with the Divine, and their standing with man, they will remain planted in the same field producing the same level of harvest.

The crucifixion of self-will and selfish desire are needed to carry the cross of eternal life and spiritual abundance. No matter what our grand goals or purposes in life may be, without great sacrifice and discipline those goals will never be achieved. Personal sacrifice and the laying down of oneself as a humble servant, is required to acquire greatness in any area of life, wealth, influence or success. If we are not willing to sow ourselves we will never reap our dreams.

We like to believe that we all suffer persecution and pain because of our great virtues or morally right standing. But until we have crucified every negative, abusive, revengeful thought or attitude toward those who harm us; we are suffering because of our own wrong ideas, actions or reactions and devices not because of our righteousness. As we prayerfully consider our sorted past and our clouded present we will come to terms with the fact that our sufferings have been provoked because of our lack of knowledge, wrong decisions, or sick, embittered responses to those around us.

Most suffering comes due to the blindness of our own failings or weaknesses. Until our eyes are opened to see that our character and mental reasoning must evolve to the place where we no longer harm others in thought or deed, we cannot claim that we are suffering because of our good moral conduct and perfection. Moral, relational, or situational failures point to the places where developmental changes are still needed in our lives.

Positive life-giving thoughts and actions will never produce death or moral decay but on the contrary, they will create prosperity, wealth and abundant blessing. Negative, harmful thoughts will always produce lack and poverty whenever and wherever they are sown. The seed thoughts we sow will produce according to their kind. What kind of seeds have you been sowing? What kind of a harvest are you expecting or desiring in your life? We reap the fruits of what we sow be they good or evil, positive or negative, creative or destructive. This is the law of seedtime and harvest.

In the natural a seed will produce a harvest once it is planted and watered. The only way to stop that seed from producing is to cut it off or dig it up, by uprooting it from the soil that provides its nutrition. The only way to stop a thought from manifesting in the mental realm is to pull down every vain imagination that exalts itself above the ways of God; repent and change your mind and do not comply to or entertain that wrong thought pattern again.

Suffering comes when we have agreed with a wrong thought or supported an unconstructive, selfish action. If you are suffering in a situation consider the possibility that you may have stepped out of harmony with God, your highest self or the best for the others in your life. Suffering is a signal that notifies us that we are headed in the wrong direction; stop, repent and turn around to achieve peace and purity. Suffering produces perseverance and a clean, pure heart by removing all moral depravity and mental impurities. Painful situations caused by the suffering associated with fiery trials come when harmony is shattered or disrupted.

Spiritual reflection on God's ways followed by repentance or changing of direction allows all the dross or impure elements in one's life to rise to the top, where it is easily examined, skimmed off and removed. When the purification process takes place with precious gold, or costly silver, the Smelter is able to see His reflection smiling back at Him in the mirroring surface of the liquid metals.

Spiritual enlightenment causes our thoughts to come from a pure heart. When our heart is pure our clean hands will only perform loving deeds and godly actions and reactions. When we walk in this heightened level of purity, transparency and righteousness the trials and suffering will cease because God's image will have been formed in us.

Blessed increase and multiplication comes when a person is enlightened by truth and remains in harmony with the Spirit of God. The measure we can be blessed comes as a result of our thoughts coming into alignment and harmony with the higher thoughts of God. Poverty, lack of possessions and a stagnant wretched existence is the byproduct of sterile inactivity, a critical, negative thought life that is full of doubt and unbelief.

One can be wealthy with worldly trappings, yet cursed with life's circumstances or health issues that never allow them to enjoy their fortune. The poor in spirit inherit the kingdom, and the gentle person inherits the earth, because goodness and mercy follow them. Their joy is made full because blessing upon blessings reign down upon their lives. Wealth and fortunate approval unite when they are utilized wisely. But, the indigent continue to fail when their mental disorder refuses to take responsibility for their own wretched existence; always pointing fingers and blaming others for their unjust burdens never realizing that their desperate life situations are really due to their own neglect, laziness and selfish indulgences.

Prosperity, health, wealth and true happiness come when a person has aligned their inner thoughts, dreams and the intents of their heart with the manifestation of their outer circumstances. One only thrives and finds true happiness when they stop feeling sorry for themselves, always wallowing in self-pity. Instead of groveling in self-absorption they search for answers to the question of, "Why have these injustices come into my life?" When they gain spiritual understanding of the things they have suffered it serves as a vehicle to reveal their hidden weaknesses. They no longer accuse others for their plight in life, but continually seek ways to improve their spiritual thoughts. They allow difficulty to become a catalyst that spiritually strengthens and physically builds them up. They progress rapidly when they discover the hidden roots of iniquity or twisted thinking that limits their possibilities. Thus uprooting sin they are able to shut the negative doors of injustice that have given poverty access to their life.

Righteousness and justice are the foundational laws that govern the universe. When we align ourselves with God's righteousness, the favor of His justice will quickly follow. When we are in right standing with God in thought and deeds all of our enemies will be at peace with us. Little changes in our thought patterns and decisions make slight changes in our life. Radical changes in our mental processes and actions will render great transformation and sudden grand changes in our life.

A destitute life that is full of confusion comes from the disease of negative, impure thoughts. Weak character is full of fear, suspicion and uncertainty resulting in a life controlled by gluttony, over indulgence and codependency that enslaves. Idle, frivolous thoughts waste time and produce a dishonest beggar; no matter what he steals or how much is given to him by others, he is never satisfied. Hateful, murderous, violent or accusatory thoughts birth injury and multiply insult. Selfishness limits friendships and self-seeking thoughts break the backs of all kinds of relationships leaving one feeling all alone, rejected, distressed, isolated, abandoned, and oppressed.

A blessed life blossoms because it is giving, caring and it unselfishly exudes thoughts of beauty, grace, mercy, compassion and kind regard for others, always placing their wellbeing before its own. A pure heart controlled by morally right, temperate intensions, empowers a decisive person to reach out to others to offer peaceful resolves to life's most difficult problems. These champions are courageous persons who have built a strong, private constitution that is full of integrity. Their industrious nature is able to formulate and wisely execute plans that succeed. Their pleasant, well-mannered, forgiving thoughts produce the genteel hero's nature that protects, watches over, guards and preserves others. Their love for all, frees them from self-centered thoughts. These are the true servants of God who easily achieve earthly prosperity and true spiritual wealth.

Whatever seed thought or ideology a person meditates upon with either excellent concentration focused upon God or evil malignant intentions alert to self desire, they will always produce the same fruit in character and harvest the identical life's circumstances without fail because life will issue from its source. Clearly nobody can completely choose the dreams that come or totally control his life circumstances, but we can choose the thoughts which will eventually shape our environment. The world around us ensures that the good thoughts, and the evil things we focus on, foster, and desire will empower a door of opportunity to surface. Then a person must make godly choices to walk the higher path of integrity or they will be trapped in the lowly miry pit of ambiguity never achieving their higher purpose, dreams or destiny.

A person must shift his thoughts from evil to good, from causing pain to blessing and supporting, from criticizing to encouraging others, then and only then will the world be kinder and soften towards them. When a person's focus is outward toward helping others, those they help will in turn reach out to thank and help them. We reap what we sow; when we respond to life in strength, instead of weakness, we sow strong seeds of abundance and plenty. When we think good thoughts towards all those we meet, they will think kind thoughts towards us, releasing the iron bonds that try to ensnare or bind us away from reaching our goals. Thus comes the saying, "Iron sharpens iron." The beautiful, brilliant or dull, drab colors that appear in the looking glass of life are an expressed reflection of our heart's moving thoughts.

Chapter 16
Thoughts Affect Our Health

We are who and what we think because the brain regulates the whole body. The body obeys and is servant to our deliberate waking thoughts as well as our subconscious thoughts of the night. Poisonous undesirable thoughts plunge the body into a weakened sickened state of disease and decay. Optimistic productive thoughts, focused on the Word of God, release the power to renew both the mind and the body with the beauty of youth. One can trace the root cause of lack and disease, as well as health and wealth, to their positive or negative thoughts and intents of the heart. Sickly thoughts poison the body, releasing toxins that sabotage various organs, muscles and joints in the body with sickness and disease. Fear, panic, stress and dread can stop someone's heart in an instant. Those who fear they will become sick, do become sick, or they die of cancer or have a heart attach, because they draw the very things they fear into their lives. Anxiety, worry and trepidation erode and ruin the whole body opening it up for weakness and disease. Crippling thoughts gallop throughout the whole body and stress the nervous system.

Happy thoughts of trust, grace and purity strengthen and invigorate the body. Our delicate anatomy responds to the effects of both pure, clear and evil, unclean thoughts and impressions. Clean life habits produce a strong, healthy body and mind. A mind that is defiled with pride or a vain, depraved imagination will corrupt the body and destroy one's life. The mind controls the pure or contaminated waters of thought that flows out of the fountain of life. Pure, clean thoughts restore the soul and body; while polluted thoughts release debris that clutters and blocks the flow of creative healing. When negative or destructive thoughts are bottled up, they form poisonous damns that stop a healthy flow and drain the body's strength.

Habitually consuming the wrong types and quantities of foods adds strain to an already weakened body. To loose weight one must change their thoughts about food and the type of calories they take into their digestive system. When a person corrects their thought life, they no longer crave the wrong types of foods. Instead of devouring junk food, white sugar and flour, cakes, potato chips, bread and rice they will consume fruits, vegetables, nuts and meat in the right portions.

Clear, pure thoughts create a whole saintly person with a clear, pure body and mind. Guard your heart and beautify the mind to obtain a perfect, whole body. Thoughts of depression, despair, sorrow, grief and despondency steal strength and health from the body producing a sad countenance. God will cause the light of His magnificent countenance to shine favor upon the serene individual who keeps his mind stayed on the precepts of God's peaceable ways and Word.

Sickness will flee when a person dwells in a continuous state of God's presence, joy, compassion and goodwill. Disease grows in an environment that is rich in heartbreaking sorrow, disappointment and grief. The prison of cynicism, suspicion and jealousy destroys hope and renders one bitter and resentful towards others. But, when one loves, forgives and thinks the best of others, patience blossoms in goodwill towards mankind releasing heaven on earth. The peace of God that passes all understanding will guard and rule one's heart towards every living being and abundant grace will flow.

Chapter 17 Thoughts Birth Purpose: As a Man Thinks so is He

Strategic goals and destinies are accomplished when our lives and thoughts revolve around Divine purpose. When thoughts are randomly scattered we continue to float aimlessly through the sea of life. To steer clear of failure and chance, one must follow God's skillful plan and discipline their thoughts to follow a clearly laid path to reach success. Destruction and catastrophe lurk in the waves for those who aimlessly drift through life not knowing their purpose or discovering their calling in life. They are easily pulled in any direction like a bobbing lure floating on the ocean waves. Without placing God first in one's life as their dominate reason for existence, one is easily distracted or coerced to serve someone else's life plan. Instead of becoming a leader, they become the follower of someone's well laid endeavors. When we are not focused on achieving the ideals we have been created to accomplish in life we are troubled with doubt, fears and worries. These negative emotions lead to an easily defeated life, filled with self-pity and envy towards others who are attractive, high achievers, goal directed, decisive and intellectually successful.

We each must birth, define, sculpt and conform to the life purpose and dream that resides in our hearts. By carefully exploring one's strengths and eliminating one's weaknesses we daily draw closer to accomplishing goals that lead to apprehending the purpose for which we were born. When spiritual purpose steers the influences in our lives we are full of joy, creativity and expectation. When we systematically focus on the next task or objective that is set before us, they are easily fulfilled. Each accomplishment does its work of forming and transforming us into the person we are destined to become. By training our mind to stay focused on God's plans, and not wandering off on rabbit trails or frivolous desires, our objectives become attainable.

Self-control is a virtue that enables the thoughts of our mind to concentrate on the task at hand. By staying focused on one task at a time, even if we continue to fail, eventually we will discover how to ascend the mountain by overtaking every enemy that comes to exploit our weaknesses. As we ascend the next step we are now closer to achieving our purpose and dreams. New strength of character, skill and imagination has developed the measure of our success. This new launching pad will enable future triumphs and empower us to achieve our goals more quickly.

Sometime failure is the best teacher because we will never repeat the same painful mistakes twice. We fall so we can learn how to pick ourselves up again. Our goal should be excellence, to accomplish each task to the best of our ability, no matter how menial that task may seem at the time. Years ago I was a Veterinarian Technician. Part of my job required me to clean dirty animal cages. I dreaded that part of my job until I decided to do it as unto the Lord to the best of my ability. Once I changed my view and attitude I no longer despised the menial part of my work and the kennel always shined.

Creative energy is a wonderful way to resolve problems; there is more than one way to achieve greatness. The least of us once discovering our weakness can exert ourselves in prayer, through diligent effort and patient long-suffering, by believing we can, we will overcome every limitation. Thus new strength is formed that will continue to develop until our divine purpose is realized. Physical, mental and spiritual strength comes by careful daily planning, coupled with exercising patient training. Thinking upon excellent things that are pure will develop a habit of right thought processes.

The person who spends their time in aimless thoughts or lazily gazes at the nonsensical programs designed by man will never join the ranks of those who achieve their God given goals. Their procrastination always delays things until tomorrow. By not taking responsibility for their failure they will never become successful. Their dreams dwindle and are in no way realized.

Those who run upon the pathway of attainment, turn every defeat into a triumph so that it always serves their ultimate purpose. Their thoughts remain strong and focused as they fearlessly master every obstacle. Their dreams are always realized over time because dreams really do come true.

When destiny is conceived, the ground work must be laid, so that the path becomes straight, enabling one to avoid the crooked ditches of doubt and the pitfalls of fear and failure. Fear brings paralysis and extinguishes a powerful purpose by draining one's creative energy. Knowledge that one can do the task at hand produces the will to accomplish their dream. While conquering doubt and shattering fear one is able to release the chains that bind and manacle us to failure and defeat. He who entertains the notion of fear will thwart his purpose. The ability to conquer the enemies of doubt, fear and unbelief means you are able to conquer failure. Power-filled thoughts and prayers enable us to bravely encounter, engage and overcome all of life's difficulties. New creative thoughts and prayerful meditations that are planted in the proper season of life will bring forth the conscious fruit of maturity and intellectual resolve.

The thoughts we think and the type of prayers we pray empower our dreams to succeed or to fail. Where we find ourselves in life is a direct result of our taking responsibility or denying responsibility for our weaknesses and faults. We are who we are, because of our own thoughts; it is not because of someone else's input or exclusion. The character flaws or strengths, chaste virtue, happiness, suffering or our object poverty are our own doings, not another's; they cannot be altered by anyone but our self. Do you know what condition your condition is in? Persecution, suffering and joy all emanate from within, as a man thinks, so is he. But more importantly as a person thinks they are, they will remain in that condition, as long as they continue to campout and think in those same patterns.

No one can help another change or develop a strong resolve in life unless that person is open to and willing to change, seeking and asking for wise guidance. If a person lacks anything, let him pray and ask God for wisdom, so their character and integrity can be enhanced. It requires a concerted effort and conscious discipline to change in order to reflect the attributes one appreciates or respects in others. No one can alter someone else; only that person, through prayer and meditating upon the Word of God and then setting godly principles into practice, can a person bring forth desired changes and obtain their dreams.

Until the ignorance that holds us captive is brought to a saving knowledge of love, both the dominated person, and the harsh dominator, afflict them. The only law that is necessary to bring forth true change is love. Where hate and evil desire prevail there is bondage that leads to murder. If a person hates themselves or another they have already afflicted, bound or murdered that person in the imagination of their heart. All that is left for them to do now is to lay their hands on them or pick up the material instrument and carry out their sorted plans of destruction. In the realm of the Spirit they are already guilty of murder.

Perfect love cast out fear of both the oppressor and the oppressed for each are suffering from a lack of knowledge. To love someone completely, one must cover the multitude of their sin and weaknesses. To think you are better or know more is to elevate yourself in a spirit of pride above another as their superior. To stay focused on self-centered thoughts is to demonstrate one's own weaknesses. To conquer the hatred one feels towards a dominator and to defeat the unction to dominate another, one must elevate their mind to constantly think loving thoughts towards others.

Love is not judgmental or rude. It thinks or believes no evil about someone else and never forces its own desire on others. Love is patient, long suffering and kind. Love brings freedom to the one who is sowing love and also to the one who is receiving love. Love brings a liberty to be oneself, but it also enables that person the freedom to change when necessary. If we do not feel loved, we will remain the same weak person residing in abject misery. When love infiltrates our environment, hope springs forth, empowering us to be healed, rise above obstacles, conquer weaknesses, and achieve impossible feats in life.

Love has the power to lift each of us to a platform where we can achieve anything in the natural and in the divine supernatural dimensions of existence. When we love God, ourselves and others, power is released within; the power of love enables us to transcend limitations. When we take our eyes off of our own selfish desires and seek the Kingdom of God first, all things positive are added to us. So by relinquishing our own desires in life, eternal life is achieved. By dying to one's self we enable a life of abundance that draws others into the Kingdom of God. The person who only considers himself continues to fail in life; he remains weak and alone. No one is drawn to a loser; but gladly supports the magnetic personality of a winner. To truly succeed one must die to their own selfish indulgence becoming a servant to all.

If a person cannot control their personal affairs, how can they center their life on benefiting others, planning ahead or be given added responsibility? In order to develop the strength of character that can stand alone and then assist others, we must first master our own thoughts, discipline our actions and then seek to reach out to lovingly benefit others. The thoughts we think will either limit or increase us. To progress in life one must first be able to sacrifice things that pertain to self.

Worldly success can be measured by one's ability to fix their mind on God's higher ways and plans, follow godly principles, and strengthen their resolve to discipline their thought life. The more we meditate on godly principles the more blessed, prosperous and successful we will become. Adopting godly principles enables spiritual growth which insures we will be able to maintain our increase longer. Before God releases multiplication He develops the strength of the person's character so they can carry and sustain the added weight of blessing.

Success can be very heavy to carry. True success is limited by the dynamics of our thoughts. Finishing well, positive developments and achievements correspond to the degree a person is willing to let go of brutish, worldly, or self-centered thoughts. The more closely we pattern our thoughts, dreams and life actions to those of God's the more He is able to prosper and bless us. Prosperity of soul, body and spirit as well as financial and physical prosperity requires discipline and sacrifice.

God does not favor the dishonest, selfish or greedy, violently aggressive, immorally unsound, or the wicked whose character grows from bad to worse, although at times it may appear as if they are prospering more than the godly. God sends the rain on the righteous and the unrighteous at the same time. Weed seeds spring up quickly but only survive a short time on the shallow stony path of self, while good virtuous seed that bring forth eternal fruit, require a depth of development that takes a long time to germinate and take root. Whatever we pursue we will find. If we seek the face of God with all of our heart He will be found of us. If we use our intellect to search out knowledge and understanding we will discover their truths. Earthly knowledge leads to the sensuality of vanity and the emptiness of ambition that stems from much toiling linked with a combination of exhaustive effort.

Spiritual wisdom comes from an awe inspired heart solely focused upon watching the beautiful face of God who has become our magnificent obsession. A pure thought life develops a well rounded, excellent character which positions a person to receive God's help and approval so their godly success can positively influence others by provoking them to jealousy. To achieve the champions wreath disciplined effort, self-control, and a single minded determination must continually direct ones thoughts upward to ascend the gradient ladder of success. When impure, arrogant, selfish, controlling or corrupt thoughts possess a soul, even for a short period of time, it leads to a descent into the poverty of confusion, depravity, weakness and error.

To maintain a humble position of spiritual virtue and wisdom one must keep a vigilant watch continually searching the issues of their heart and guarding the thoughts of their mind or they will rapidly plummet back into the mire of decay, depression and failure. All social status whether academic, commercial or spiritual comes from thoughts governed by godly principles and commandments. When we follow God's precepts and laws they are written upon the tablets of our heart. As a man's heart beats so he lives and moves and has the essence of his being in God. When the heart is full of God's love and grace great things are accomplished. When the heart is eclipsed by one's own selfish desires and agendas nothing of eternal value happens, no matter how many talents a person may possess. The more one dies to self the more they will achieve. Except a man lay down his life for others, he will remain isolated and alone, sacrifice is required for real success.

Chapter 18
Dreams Set the Standards of the World

Visionary dreamers gaze into the invisible realms of God. Infused with God's wisdom their imagination grasps the magnitude of the impossible. As they continue to seek God, fresh promises are released that enable them to solve devastating world situations. The solitary prophet, a seer, or the dreamer of dreams, who dares to discover truth, believes the promises of God. They understand the hidden mysteries of divine wisdom, which are positioned in the imperceptible realms of glory. They know that through godly understanding, their faith is enlightened so that they can make knowledge become evident to solve any earthly quandary.

The world reveres the dreamer, the maker of the now, and the creator of the thereafter, the spiritual architect who builds heaven on earth. We cherish their ability to gather ingenious truths, access realms of creative imagination that empowers them to execute ideals and sage-like wisdom which flow from heaven's glorious throne.

Such divine knowledge comes to reside in the hearts of those who dare to believe that with God's creative ability nothing is impossible. Poets script words that causes the heart to sing liberty's chorus. The delicate strokes of the painter's brush captures the myriad of colors memorializing abstract figures on her canvas. The composer joins melody and music to form an orchestra that frees the soul of man to worship a magnificent God. The sculptor listens to the melodies of eternal life and releases a masterpiece of beauty that has been concealed in a marble tomb with every precise blow of the chisel directed by his skilled hand. These artisans are the seers of the future; those who know the invisible hope as a clear reality of today. Humanity is beautifully blessed because their lives enrich ours; without their spiritual hunger for God's face we would famish.

It is wisdom to cherish God above all, as first and foremost in every area of your life. He will abundantly prosper you. Value and esteem the unseen visions of God as realities that form your brilliant thoughts. Holding a heavenly ideal as dear to the heart will enable the unattainable dream to come forth with bold clarity.

Love draws the spiritual world of matchless beauty, faultless peace, material wealth and the wonderful people we treasure toward us. God sees each one of us as altogether lovely. God clothes us with robes of His righteousness. He stirs our heart with passion and forms purity within our minds as we are transformed into His divine image.

The building blocks of revelation come out of quietly basking in God's luminous presence. Meditating on His beauty and majesty brings about a divine exchange. The Holy Spirit takes our disappointing ashes and gives us His magnificence to sculpt our earthly environment, and transforming our body into His heavenly habitation. Who and what are you drawing into your life? What type of spiritual habitation are you designing? To hope in God is to attain; to seek Him is to acquire. If we focus on the little, thinking the grand is out of our reach, we will receive nothing but loss. But, if we allow a pure heart to imagine magnificence we will be lavishly fulfilled. Ask and you shall receive, knock and the door will be opened to you, seek and you shall find. Wise men daily seek God with all their heart. A heart that first seeks the kingdom of God is a heart that will obtain the impossible.

Dream the impossible and become the bridge that brings the possibilities of future promise into the reality of now. Guard and possess the vision of what you will one day be deep within in your heart. Prophecy life, breath, increase and multiplication until at last the veil is removed revealing the new you, the handiwork of God's masterpiece. Dreams are the seeds of reality that script a person's highest destiny. The impossible, an unexplored desire, was once an ethereal dream vapor encapsulated in the shadows of a future time. With diligent thought, prayerful meditations, planning and hard work your concealed ideals come forth to manifest life's greatest achievement.

The magnificent oak tree with its expansive reaching arms of shade was once bound, held captive in the walls of a small acorn. The mother bird patiently waits, gently perched upon a nest full of fragile incubating eggs. She is expectant and assured her young will one day emerge to fly. The next generation of intellectual genius', world leaders, problem solvers and spiritual mystics were all once lovingly held within the protective chamber of their mother's resilient womb. Those who reached the fullness of their developmental term are birthed to have a chance of reaching their God given destiny. But what happens to the children, who were aborted for convenience sake, selfishly sacrificed on the altar of expediency and now? They will never reach their rightful place in society. The tragic loss of these individuals create a vacuum of hero's who champion God's cause; so lawless corruption continues, unrestrained as great men and women are cut down before they can breathe, crawl, or walk out their life's destiny. These unsung heroes who are carried on angels wings to heavens gates can only talk of the plans God had placed within each of them. Heaven bows its head in silence, the angels weep and the world continues to cry out in desperation for answers. While the person God created and sent with the creative gifts, skills and expressed abilities to answer their prayers and dreams was extracted from the womb, extinguished, laid to rest, and their little infant body was planted deep within the four walls of a tomb.

Death brings finality, an end to our existence in this earthly dimension, but begins our new journey in the spiritual realms beyond. When one season comes to an abrupt end, another one begins to blossom. When one generation grows old and dies, a new generation is born, thus the cycle of life continues.

Dreams bring forth new life and possibilities. Dreams when believed and followed will change a negative circumstance to a positive opportunity. Dreams cause lack to disappear and open the doors for provision to come. Dream strategies of multiplication ignite new ideals, when they are diligently worked; the wealth they release reaches abundance and overflows into prosperity. Negative circumstances can not remain when dreams are embraced and implemented. When the dream within a person moves them to productivity they must not remain the same but answer the magnitude of the call.

Everyone is motivated by the story of the determined, self-sacrificing, single mother who works three dead-end jobs to provide food, clothes and shelter for her little children that she so desperately loves. Though exhausted, she continues to dream, pray and develops the God given strategy for success into the wee hours of the morning. She applies herself to imagining what life would be like when she apprehends the vision and masters the economic expansion she was shown in God's visions of the night. She develops every aspect of the revelation which inspires the development of a new powerful self-image.

She sheds the destitute reflection of a victim's mentality and no longer agrees with her current life situation. The women she once was, no longer exists in her mind, so the prison of poverty and lack can no longer restrain her. She awakes to a new day. She gathers her plans and projections in arm, rises up and sets actions to her prayers by sharing her dream with a person of influence. The door of opportunity opens wide and God's favor shines through. Her ideas are placed in motion because of her faith in God, strength of integrity and positive work ethic. She owned her dream, took responsibility for it and birthed success; no longer limited to poverty or enslaved to long hours of manual labor and non-profitable toil. Though uneducated the time she spent in the presence of God has refined her intelligence, her quick wit, and God's grace allows her inner brilliance to widen and move to the forefront.

She was born to inspire others to remold their character until it reflects God's greatness. Through positive change, continued discipline and sacrifice countless lives now revolve around the center of the idea God gave her to produce a life of abundance. By obeying the dreams God sent, she has become the master of her destiny and is granted the power and honor to enable others to reach their destiny too. She rises from the pit of obscurity to a place of prominence. Those who see her success recognize her as a woman who spends countless hours in the presence of God. Heaven's favor and bountiful grace shines God's sustaining strength and benevolence upon her all the days of her life.

We will realize our destiny when we grasp the God given vision with both hands as if grasping a plow. Once securely anchored in Christ's call we keep our eyes focused on the future goal that which we love, and continue to walk step by step, pressing forward, until we have plowed through every obstacle, removed every rock of offense, and have uprooted every weed that threatens our dream.

Surrendering to that which we love and think about the most will cause a gravitational pull upon the strings of our heart. We obtain the harvest of what we produce in both thought and deed, reaping what we have sown. Our harvest will remain, change, decrease, increase, or multiply with the dimensions of our belief structures and visionary thoughts. We produce according to the thoughts we think. We will evolve into our greatest hope or diminish to the degree we allow sin to control our desires. That is why we should always keep our hope centered on Christ Jesus. He never disappoints and always does exceedingly abundantly, above and beyond our wildest thoughts and imagination.

Success takes hard work and sacrifice. The narrow-minded equate a person's wealth or prosperity to chance, fortune or the fate of providence. They have no idea or knowledge of the years of intense struggle and immense sacrifices that person has made to walk where they walk. They think she is lucky or just favored by God. They have no understanding of the intensity of the process, but only observe the glorious result and call it Divine intervention.

Envy does not grasp the vast amount of faith it took to overcome the varied trials and test. Nor does jealousy understand the great effort the successful individual had to exert to gain the experiences that are necessary to mold their pristine character. The undaunted efforts of the successful person prepared them to handle an enormous increase of influence, authority, fame and power. The casual onlooker does not see the darkness of heartache, deep pain and suffering that came before the bright noonday sun arose on their vision. The casual observer has no regard for the turmoil that was experienced by the achiever on their demanding passage to acquire their life's dream, so they call it good fortune.

Everything we do requires diligence and effort to gain either a positive or a negative outcome. The amount of effort that is needed is determined by the strength of their outcome. The fruits of our efforts determine the level of our skill development, the accuracy or the level of power our gift contains and the measure of our physical, mental and spiritual control. These are all results of the thoughts we think, the goals we achieve and the dream we finally live. The dream you hold the dearest will become the divine blue print and the model your heart follows. The things and people we allow in our lives will mold us into their image. Their presence will eventually give us the tools that are needed to build our life so we can evolve into a person of destiny or they will tear us down.

Chapter 19
Tranquility

There is nothing more beautiful than walking hand in hand with the one you love by a tranquil body of shimmering water gazing at the mirrored reflection of the stars as they frame the golden moon. The fresh air brings peace to one's mind and serenity of heart enabling contemplation of thought while pondering produces gems of wisdom.

Precious jewels are formed beneath the earth's surface through many years of patient effort and concentrated pressure. As we learn to practice patience and possess self-control the jewels of wisdom and the prosperity that God grants us increase. We find that we prosper to the measure that our soul prospers. Life experiences avail us to a wealth of practical knowledge. If we embrace a positive attitude we are empowered to move forward to victory. However, if we focus on the negative aspects of a situation our energy is drained causing us to stall and stumble. The things we focus on and allow our thoughts to dwell upon be they positive or negative will either empower us for success or insure our continued failure.

You have heard it said that knowledge is power. The more we know about ourselves the more at peace with ourselves we can become. Understanding why we do certain things or react in certain ways allows us to make the necessary adjustments to rise to a higher place of existence in God. Once we understand ourselves and see ourselves the way God sees us, we begin the process of understanding the internal principles of cause and effect that arises from those who surround us.

When we can discern why people say the things they do and act the way they act, we will cease from striving, fussing, arguing, or constantly trying to change people. Embrace people for who they are in the moment. This frees us to rejoice in knowing and loving them for who they are right now. By removing future expectations of a certain action, response or performance from that person we allow ourselves to move in unswerving, balanced peace always maintaining a tranquil spirit.

The serene person remains at peace because they both understand and control the thoughts that dwell within them. They are able to cast down vain imaginations that go against the knowledge of God. Anything that is contrary to God's purpose, plan or expression is removed from their thought processes. They will not entertain poisonous or negative thoughts. They only think on that which is pure, positive, helpful and useful to edify them or others. The serene person is able to lovingly embrace others and adjusts themselves according to others' responses. They understand that the outward actions of others are the result of them responding to their secret thoughts. Serenity and quiet observation enables us to remain teachable, knowing that we are capable of learning from those around us.

People are drawn to a calm person who has developed a spiritual clarity and depth. The expanse of their strength and their spiritual deepness becomes evident when difficulties arise. People rely upon them for wisdom and guidance in various life situations. The more peace that is resident within a person the greater the measures of influence, power, prestige and success they will manifest. People revere and seek out a tranquil self-controlled, confident person. When you honor and treat all people with respect they will gravitate toward you and give you preference over others.

A person of strong character and exquisite integrity will always be admired and loved. A person of honor will govern themselves well in every area of life. They are like a huge oak tree of righteousness whose branches stretch out to shade others from the noon day sun. They are like an immovable boulder that is steadfast and steady when the winds blow and the waves of life rages against it they remain unaffected, an anchor that brings stability and hope to others.

People of moral fiber have a sweet giving spirit, a tranquil balanced heart and live a well rounded life. They seek to serve and bless others. The honest person remains steadfast and secure comes what may; difficult circumstances and negative trying situations do not rattle their confidence in God. The person with a godly disposition remains calm, composed and peaceful day in and day out. The joy of the Lord sustains them. They know and have a quiet assurance that no matter what trials may test their endurance God will turn every tide for their good.

Tranquility is the fruit that develops in a soul that is at rest in God's peace. This peace passes all the realms of our earthly understanding. Peace and serenity are precious jewels that adorn saintly actions. They can be compared to wisdom and purity; which are more desirable than great riches or costly gold. To possess all the money in the world yet loose the peace of one's soul would be of no value. A good life can be measured by the amount of peace one possesses. If tranquility is missing there will be no happiness or fruitfulness. Without serenity the desires of the heart will never be realized only torment, sorrow and pain. A peaceful life of truth is more valuable than great riches and wealth beyond comprehension.

There was a wealthy man who although married never knew tranquility or true love from either his wife or his children. For many years he tried to hold his family together while his growing business and grueling travel schedule demanded his presence. He earned an amazing level of success so he gave large amounts of money to support their extravagant life styles and the shopping habit his family had developed. To entertain herself and contend with her loneliness during his extended periods of absence, the wife began abusing food and drugs. Eventually she became so depressed, delusional and self-absorbed that she filed for a legal separation, purchased, decorated and moved into another home. Having lived in a separate home for years, she finally filed for divorce demanding half of his estate. Even after the highly publicized divorce was finalized, his ex-wife kept him tied up in court for years demanding more houses, jewelry and increased amounts of alimony and spending money while his broken heart continued to suffer from the ravages of divorce. He only heard from his now grown, married children and the ex-wife when they wanted more material gain from him.

As time passed and the years rolled by he continued the long painful process of emotional recovery. Though he was always surrounded by people, he had no one to love or call his own; he was very lonely, even in a crowd. He prayed that God would send him an extraordinary friend and godly companion to love and comfort him. He made his desires known each morning in prayer. He wanted a special someone to love and enjoy the rest of his life with. One bright day God answered his prayer. He met the beautiful woman of his dreams. She was everything he had ever hoped for and more than he had dreamed possible. They were soul mates and compatible in every way. They were inseparable spending all their time together laughing and serving the Lord. They fell deeply in love with each other during a fairytale whirlwind romance, got engaged and planned to marry. They loved each other more than life. An engagement ring was secured and a wedding was planned.

Although he had never been so happy, his ex-wife and children opposed the marriage. Love would have wanted him to marry his greatest happiness. But tragically, instead of fighting for his true love, he yielded to the tyranny of his family's control. He needlessly sacrificed true love and tranquility for a temporary peace that would only last as long as he submitted to the family's desires, selfish control, and manipulation. Once his true love was expelled, he once again filled his travel schedule to help manage his heartbreak and empty life. He conformed to the cruelty of an old familiar mold that stole any hope for his personal happiness. Instead of embracing the fiancé who would have insured that his life would have been happily extended, and prospered, by him protecting the adoring lady God had blessed him with, he lost the one person who would have given him the ability to regain all the love he had lost. He could have lived a peaceable life of tranquility surrounded by her love and support. Instead he substituted true love and peace for a false temporary peace. Only God's blessing will bring sustainable peace everything else is fleeting vanity.

Unthinking egotistic people rush forward with unrestrained passions that cause tumultuous waves of grief, pain and multiplied sorrows in other's lives and relationships. They do not realize that their actions are altering someone's happiness. Destiny can be compromised when someone pushes their selfish desires onto someone else. Self-centeredness causes suffering, fear and doubt to arise on every wave. A bold wise person who places their confidence in God will not be overcome by the manipulation or fear tactics of others. They will guard the affections of their hearts and purify the thoughts of their minds until the winds that rage around them are quieted with peace when godly wisdom reigns in their lives.

There is hope for the storm ravaged soul who is weighted down by the cares of this world, who succumb to angry, jealous individuals that are impossible to please, yet they continue to hammer and force their agenda pressing their influence to its full measure. The realms of God's blessing and peace await your arrival. It only requires a quiet contemplation and reflection upon His Word and entering into the Holy Spirit's presence with thanksgiving. Recount the wonderful things God has done for you. Allow a grateful heart of peace to override the critical barrage of others. Renew your mind with the continual washing of God's Word. Keep your hand upon the sword of thought to slay every evil, negative, contrary thought of doubt, or unbelief.

You have been called to greatness. Awaken the inner strength of self-control. Master every thought that God has given by coating it with the Word of God. Remain calm and reserved, serenity will allow peace to rule supreme in your life. Be still and know that God is present, make Him Lord of every area of your life. Enter in at the narrow gate and reside in the calm assurance of Divine peace. Then you will see the invisible face of God.

End Notes

1. Page 7 The Temptation of Jesus from page 231, Dream Encounters Seeing Your Destiny from God's Perspective

2. Page 46 Gnosis, Strong's NT:1108 from NT:1097; knowing (the act), i.e. (by implication) knowledge: KJV - knowledge, science.

3. Page 46 Epignosis, Strong's NT:1922), acknowledge a full, or thorough knowledge, discernment, recognition.

4. Page 46 Apokalypsis, the Greek meaning "an unveiling" or "a disclosure." (from Bible Knowledge Commentary/Old Testament Copyright © 1983, 2000 Cook Communications Ministries; Bible Knowledge Commentary/New Testament Copyright © 1983, 2000 Cook Communications Ministries. All rights reserved.)

5. Page 46 Yada: Strong's Genesis 4:1, OT: 3045(Biblesoft's New Exhaustive Strong's Numbers and Concordance with Expanded Greek-Hebrew Dictionary. Copyright © 1994, 2003, 2006 Biblesoft, Inc. and International Bible Translators, Inc.)

6. Page 81 A. W. Tozer "The Knowledge of the Holy" Page 6-7 published Harper Collins Publishers, 10 East 53rd Street, New York 1002, Copyright 1961.

7. Page 79-111 Segments on the Seer were taken from GATEWAY to the SEER REALM Look Again to See Beyond the Natural Copyright ©2012 Published by Barbie Breathitt Enterprises, LLC

8. Page 114 Quote from Dream Encounters Seeing Your Destiny from God's

Perspective by Barbie L. Breathitt Chapter 2 Page 24 Published by Barbie Breathitt Enterprises, LLC Copyright© 2009

9. Page 118 Created: OT: Strongs 1254, HEBREW bara' (baw-raw'); means to create as a creator; to select or decide to cut down; to choose to continue to feed as a formative process: to make fat.

10. Page 118 Formed: OT: Strongs 3335, HEBREW yatsar (yaw-tsar'); to form, fashion, frame, make or mold something earthen through squeezing it into shape especially as a potter molds the clay into a useful or beautiful vessel; figuratively, to determine to, place purpose into, (to form a resolution).

Author Bio

Dr. Barbie L. Breathitt is a certified Prophetic Dream Life Coach, an author, ordained minister, dedicated educator, a gifted spiritual Seer, and respected teacher of the Divine supernatural manifestations of God. Barbie's dynamic teaching skills, intelligence, and quick wit make her a favorite with audiences everywhere. Through prayer, intense study, and years of research, Barbie has become the recognized leader in dream interpretation and has equipped people in more than 40 nations around the globe. Her prophetic gifting and deep spiritual insights have helped multiplied thousands of people understand the diverse ways God speaks to us today. Barbie has degrees from Southeastern University and Abraham Baldwin Agricultural College. Barbie earned her Ph.D. from Tabernacle Bible College and Seminary. Through her tangible faith and motivating life stories, Barbie challenges her audience to dive into the deeper mysteries of God with the anticipation of hearing His voice clearly and experiencing the touch of His presence. Her desire is to span denominational boundaries and bridge the gap between the secular realm of truth seekers with a clear message of hope, signs, and wonders, and the demonstration of the power of God. Her passion in life is to help individuals pursue their understanding of a loving God and to find their highest purpose and destiny in Him.

Coming Soon!

DreamsDecoder.com

Dr. Barbie Breathitt is a Certified Life Coach and will be available for personal coaching sessions soon!

If you'd like to know when the site is launched, please join our email list found at www.myonar.com to receive our monthly newsletters.